Living Words in Philippians

LIVING WORDS IN PHILIPPIANS

Wayne Detzler

EVANGELICAL PRESS

EVANGELICAL PRESS
16/18 High Street, Welwyn, Hertfordshire,
AL6 9EQ, England

© Evangelical Press 1984

First published 1984

ISBN 0 85234 183 0

Unless otherwise stated, all Bible quotations are from the New International Version.

Also available in this series by Wayne Detzler:

LIVING WORDS IN 1 CORINTHIANS
LIVING WORDS IN EPHESIANS
LIVING WORDS IN 1 PETER

Cover Design by Peter Wagstaff
Typeset in Great Britain by Inset, Chappel, Essex
Printed by The Pitman Press, Bath, England

*To Rev. and Mrs E. F. Partridge
for their godly influence as
pastor and parents-in-law*

Contents

			Page
1.	Overlooked overseers	Phil. 1:1	11
2.	Thank-you note	Phil. 1:3	15
3.	The best defence	Phil. 1:7	19
4.	Songs of praise	Phil. 1:11	23
5.	Chain reaction	Phil. 1:13,14	27
6.	Preaching power	Phil. 1:15	31
7.	Dead end	Phil. 1:20	35
8.	Fresh fruit	Phil. 1:22	39
9.	Agony and ecstasy	Phil. 1:27,30	43
10.	Mind set	Phil. 2:2	47
11.	In form	Phil. 2:6,7	51
12.	Famous names	Phil. 2:9,10	55
13.	Powerful presence	Phil. 2:12	59
14.	Bent world	Phil. 2:15	63
15.	Keep in touch	Phil. 2:19,23,28	67
16.	Soldier on	Phil. 2:25	71
17.	Watch out	Phil. 3:2	75
18.	Gains and losses	Phil. 3:7	79
19.	Divine dynamic	Phil. 3:10	83
20.	Caught by Christ	Phil. 3:12,13	87
21.	Perfect people	Phil. 3:12,15	91
22.	Sobbing saints	Phil. 3:18	95
23.	Political preference	Phil. 3:20	99
24.	Winner's crown	Phil. 4:1	103
25.	Plea for peace	Phil. 4:2	107
26.	Joy way	Phil. 4:4	111
27.	Prayer power	Phil. 4:6	115
28.	The whole truth	Phil. 4:8	119
29.	Horn of plenty	Phil. 4:12	123
30.	The incomparable Christ	Phil. 4:13	127
31.	Yes, please	Phil. 4:18	131
32.	God's glory	Phil. 4:19,20	135

Preface

Like its three predecessors, this little volume arises out of the systematic exposition of Scripture at Kensington Baptist Church in Bristol. The four short chapters of this epistle flew by all too rapidly, especially because they marked the end of our ministry with the dear friends at Bristol.

As in the other volumes, we have isolated a Greek word, which is then studied in the context of Philippians. A second section expands the understanding of our word in the remaining New Testament books. Two invaluable aids in these studies are Robert Young's *Analytical Concordance to the Bible* and Gingrinch and Danker's English edition of Walter Bauer's *Greek-English Lexicon of the New Testament and Other Early Christian Literature*. As always, the English quotations are taken from the *New International Version* of the Bible.

Patiently my wife Margaret has plodded through the manuscript sorting out my scribal errors. Finally our dear friend Mrs Vi Williams hammered my messy manuscript into a presentable form. Of course, I must also thank the entire Kensington congregation for helping me to learn the lessons of Philippians, which we now share with you.

Wayne Detzler
Bristol

1.
Overlooked overseers

'Together with the overseers and deacons' (Phil. 1:1)

The word 'overseer' conjures up in my mind a picture of rough authority. He is the foreman on a building site, who shuffles around in an open-necked shirt, trousers with baggy knees, and perpetually scuffed shoes. Perched atop untidy hair is a hard hat designed to fend off falling bricks, or maybe even thrown ones.

Most surely this was not the picture in Paul's mind as he penned Philippians. He remembered the colonial Christians in Philippi and the men who moved among them as pastors or elders. These were simply shepherds caring for the Christian flock. Bishop Handley Moule (1841–1920), the Cambridge don and biblical scholar, saw in this phrase 'the distinctive functions of the Christian ministry ... the natural origin of the titles by which Christian ministers are designated.'[1] It is the work of an overseer which sets the tone for this study.

The Greek word translated 'overseer' is *episkopos*. It finds a reflection in such English terms as 'episcopacy' (the rule of a church by bishops) or 'episcopal' (pertaining to bishops). In the New Testament the word describes local church leaders variously known as 'elder', 'bishop', 'pastor', 'undershepherd', and even 'teacher'.

In Philippians 1:1, the 'overseers' are linked with deacons, who seem to have cared for the organizational details of church life. By contrast, the overseers were charged with the pastoral care of the congregation. Any effort to elevate elders/overseers while degrading deacons does violence to the Greek text. Paul places them on an equal level: 'overseers and deacons'.

11

In the small scope available in this book, we shall define 'overseers' by a series of contrasts. First, 'overseers' refer *not to an office, but to an occupation*. No Greeks bearing bishops' mitres strutted through the streets of Philippi in A.D. 62 (the approximate date of this epistle). 'Overseers' were not so much officials as they were elder brothers caring for Christians and guarding them from withering want and doctrinal deviation. It was the care of individuals that occupied overseers in the first century.

Second, the attitude of overseers was *not tyrannical, but tender*. They were not 'big shots' in the church, ecclesiastical canons. Today many assume titles and trappings of tyranny. These stand out in bold contrast to the early Christian overseers whose tenderness was proverbial.

Third, biblical overseers were *not regional, but local*. As *episkopos* developed into 'bishop' the bearers broadened their sphere of influence from one congregation to include all the churches in a given region. However, New Testament overseers were committed to one single church in a given town or city. This pattern of pastoral care limited to one congregation is accepted by almost all biblical commentators, even a bishop like Handley Moule.

No doubt about it, Paul here points to a function which is overwhelming in its importance. When I assumed the 'oversight' of Kensington Baptist Church an esteemed elder brother gave good advice. 'If anyone wants to hear your ministry,' my mentor admonished, 'let them come to Bristol. Stay close to your congregation.' 'Overseers' at Philippi were closely connected with their charges. That is why the apostle Paul lumps them together in one greeting with 'all the saints' and their co-labourers the deacons.

Busy bishops

'Overseer' evolved into the office of 'bishop' by the second century. In fact, 'bishop' derives from the Latin word *biscopus*, a shortened form of the Greek word *episkopos*. Those well-meaning Romans were always twisting good Greek words into Latin lingo!

Overlooked overseers

It was Ignatius (died 98/117) who always advertised bishops as a bulwark against heresy. Bishop Leo of Rome (about 400—461) warded off Attila the Hun when he came to attack the city in 452. Three years later Leo also sent the barbarian vandals packing. No wonder he became known as Leo the Great! He was a lion-hearted bishop, and he helped make Bishops of Rome into popes.

The elevation of overseers to ostentatious bishops was a post-biblical development. Pastors pushed forward one of their number and gave him the title of 'bishop' or 'overseer'. 'It originated, however, in a human custom', according to Calvin, 'and rests on no Scripture authority.'[2]

Predictably our word 'overseer' has two major meanings in the New Testament. First, it refers to *Christ*. He is viewed as 'the Shepherd and Overseer of your souls' (1 Peter 2:25). Tied to the teaching of the Good Shepherd is the task of care and comfort. By implication all other soul-snatchers are pests, prowling about to devour (1 Peter 5:8). Only Christ can keep the most valuable of all human possessions, the eternal soul.

Peter applies this truth to salvation, by which we 'return to the Shepherd and Overseer of our souls'. However, the Christian also finds repose and regular renewal under the oversight of the Overseer. Well do I recall my first summer away from home. As a teenage lad I had never coped without a strong scriptural church and solid spiritual parents. During that summer I learned that Christ was adequate to care for my soul and sustain me through his Word.

The second application is to the *church*. Eliezer the priest was commissioned with the 'charge [oversight] of the entire tabernacle and everything in it' (Num. 4:16). When we cross over into the New Testament, we encounter elders who are commanded by Paul to 'guard yourselves and all the flock of which the Holy Spirit has made you overseers' (Acts 20:28). Such an overseer, according to Paul, must be above reproach (1 Tim. 3:2). High standards are set for aspirants to the office of overseer (1 Tim. 3:1—7; Titus 1:5—9).

Few bishops today tally with the Bible picture of

overseers. One looks back longingly to Latimer, Ridley and Ryle. These and their spiritual kin combined the title of bishop with true oversight of their charges. My heart leapt lately to hear a latter-day bishop/overseer urge a young vicar to be a zealous 'fisher of men'.

Our word 'overseer' or *episkopos* is used in the New Testament to describe the work of true overseers. The writer of Hebrews speaks of those who 'see to it [exercise oversight] that no one misses the grace of God' through a bitter attitude (Heb. 12:15). God's visitation (oversight) exemplifies the protection or care that a true overseer must exercise (Luke 19:44; 1 Peter 2:12). God's providential presence is described to Moses, and the Greek Old Testament uses our word *episkope*.

In a ruthless world overseers are a welcome change. They are people who are charged by God to look out for those incapable of looking out for themselves. Never dare we let the title of overseer/elder/bishop blind us to the real business of pastoral care. To put it in Peter's words: 'Be shepherds of God's flock that is under your care, serving as overseers' (1 Peter 5:2).

1. H. G. Moule, *Philippian Studies*, p. 25 note 1.
2. J. Calvin, *Commentaries on the Epistles of Paul the Apostle to The Philippians, Colossians and Thessalonians*, p. 23.

2.
Thank-you note

'I thank my God every time I remember you' (Phil. 1:3)

The dark side of Christmas for a child is the obligatory 'thank-you note'. No sooner has the wrapping paper wrinkled onto the floor, than the nagging starts. 'Write to Auntie Gertrude. Thank her for those lovely, thick woolly socks.'

'But I don't like pea-green socks,' protests the poor recipient, 'and anyway, they don't go with anything I've got.'

'Don't be silly,' Mum takes up the argument. 'Auntie Gertrude loves you and she knitted them for you.'

Finally the harassed youngster writes in large letters for few words:

Dear Auntie Gertrude,
    Thank you for the woolly socks. They are a very unusual colour, and they will fit as soon as I grow into them. The next time it snows I may wear them.
                  Love and kisses,
                    Jennifer.

Such thank-you notes are sheer torture to write and not much more pleasant to receive. When the Bible writers thought of thanks they were sincere and spiritually inspired. No person pushed them to say 'thank you'; they were thankful.

The Greek word for giving thanks is *eucharisteo*. It has been captured by liturgical Christians and used to denote the Lord's Supper, the Eucharist. Actually the Greek root is a combination of two words: *eu*, meaning 'good or well' as in 'eulogy' (a good word), and *charizomai*, meaning 'to give freely', as in 'charisma' (God's grace gift). Together we have 'eucharist', a 'good offering of thanks'.

In the short Philippian letter the word 'thanks' turns up twice. First it is found where Paul declares, 'I thank my God every time I remember you' (Phil. 1:3). In fact, Paul waxes lyrical at this point as he throws around large generalizations. He thanks *every* time, for *every* Christian (v. 4), and *every* time he is filled with joy (v. 4). The words tumble over each other in a cascade of Spirit-inspired excitement. When compared to the gloom of Galatians or 1 Corinthians, this passage is a rousing chorus of joy to the Lord for individual believers. Every pastor gives thanks for his members. One thinks of the stalwarts who keep going for God through the decades. Then there are the eager new Christians who approach worship as if it were feeding time at the local birds' nest, mouths open and pens at the ready for any new insight into the Word. There are also the needy souls whose very vulnerability draws out the love of the church. For these and many more the pastor prays thankfully.

The second appearance of our word is in Philippians 4:6, where we are instructed in the practice of prayer: 'Do not be anxious about anything, but in everything, by prayer and petition, with thanksgiving, present your requests to God.' In his simple little devotional commentary, Guy King, the Anglican preacher and writer, summed up the verse in three short phrases: 'careful for nothing, prayerful for everything, thankful for anything'.

John Henry Jowett (1864–1923) finished his ministry in the pulpit of Westminster Chapel. To Jowett thankfulness was an essential complement to Christian living. In fact he wrote that 'Every virtue divorced from thankfulness is maimed and limps along the spiritual road.'

Sadly there are many doctrinally straight Christians who have lost the lustre of thankfulness. Consequently they are miserable specimens of spiritual stagnation. Their minds are keen with spiritual precision, but their hearts are about as warm as frozen fish fingers, and a lot less appealing. Thankfulness lifts our eyes to the majesty of our Master, from whose hand every good thing comes.

Thank you very much

When some say, 'Thank you very much', it is sarcastic and sour. But the Bible never twists thankfulness. It is always genuine and gentle.

Thankfulness is directed by divine revelation into proper channels. First, there is thanks for *food*. When Jesus broke up a boy's lunch to feed five thousand, he first thanked the Father (John 6:11). Paul also gave thanks when sea-sick mariners took their first nourishment (Acts 27:35). Overseas holidays have added a new dimension to thanksgiving. True blue Britons only grudgingly give thanks for exotic, explosively spiced Spanish or Greek dishes. When they return home their thanks for fish and chips are much more enthusiastic!

A second focus for thanksgiving is *Christian companions*. Paul gave thanks for the Romans, who were under fire (Rom. 1:8), the Colossians, who were confused (Col. 1:3) and the Thessalonians, who were puzzled by death (1 Thess. 1:2). No matter how troublesome his spiritual offspring were, Paul still thanked God for them. When we first arrived in Germany as missionaries we were thrown together with a wildly divergent corps of Christian workers. After the initial euphoria wore off, we lapsed into chronic criticism. Only in later years could we come to give thanks for and ultimately lovingly respect our colleagues.

The third reason for thanksgiving is *miracles*. The Samaritan who was healed of leprosy by the Lord returned to give thanks (Luke 17:16). Miracles make us thankful, especially when we benefit from them.

Part of the liberating work of the Holy Spirit is seen when we give thanks for miracles in other people's lives. The next door Baptist church has enjoyed unusual response to the gospel, and we give thanks with that brother in the ministry. One of my closest friends preaches every Sunday to capacity crowds, and we give thanks for him. Now that is not easy. Frequently my frustrated little ego screams out: 'Why do those fellows get all the breaks?' Because this reaction is so blatantly unbiblical I say it only to my study wall, my long-suffering dog and my equally patient readers. Thanks are God's will. The complaint of a petty pastor is not God's plan.

A final occasion for thanks is the *Lord's Table*. The symbol of our Lord's blood is called by Paul 'the cup of thanksgiving for which we give thanks' (1 Cor. 10:16). In the words of institution reference is likewise made to the Lord's giving thanks (1 Cor. 11:24). In other words, the Lord's Table cannot be separated from thanksgiving. We do not call it the 'eucharist', but we still give thanks each time for his table. When we settled along the south coast of England we joined a small Baptist church. Each time we came to the Lord's Table a frail, unsteady 'life deacon' was led to the front. When he stood to give thanks his ninety years seemed to fall away. His voice resounded with youth and his speech sparkled clear as crystal. He did not hear us very well, but he was surely heard by the God he worshipped and thanked.

We do not always know what is right. It is not always clear whether or not we should move. What we should say is not known in every situation. But there is one word which should never be far from our lips. It is 'thanks'. 'Give thanks in all circumstances, for this is God's will for you in Christ Jesus' (1 Thess. 5:18).

3.
The best defence

> 'Defending *and confirming the gospel*' (Phil. 1:7)

Defence smells of defeat. In recent years the Swedes have had to defend their neutral shores from sneaking Soviet submarines. Defence is devoted to maintaining their position on the fence between East and West.

In sport we learn that the best defence is a good offence. If a football team lolls around its own goal, sooner or later the opposition is going to grace the back of the net with the ball. Only when the team takes its attack to the other end is their goal really safe.

The word translated in the New International Version with 'defending' is a Greek word *apologeomai*. It is also found in noun form, *apologia*. Its closest English relative is 'apology' or 'apologize'. Of course, in English this carries the connotation of 'bowing and scraping', acknowledging that one has made a blunder and begging pardon. In Greek the word simply signified defence, and was most at home in a court of law.

Twice our word crops up in Philippians. In his introduction Paul proclaims that he is 'in chains . . . defending and confirming the gospel' (Phil. 1:7). This is a negative idea. He is fighting off the attacks of Roman officials against the gospel. They are not attacking because of their devotion to Nero worship. Rather they are enforcing a public order act. Paul has been charged with raising the roof in Jerusalem (Acts 21:30–32).

Defence to Paul meant removing man-made obstacles to the gospel, arguing the reasonableness of the gospel before potential or real opposers. The same is seen today in the public debate concerning creation. Not many will be persuaded to believe by debate, but it may make some think. After all, there is an intelligent alternative to Darwin's fairy tale. Christians are convinced that an intelligent cause for creation is far superior to blind chance and a crack-up in the molecule race. (Evolutionists actually *believe* that everything emerged from a collision between molecules a very long time ago. What faith!)

Paul presents a second glimpse of our word in Philippians. From Nero's Roman mad-house Paul writes, 'I am put here for the defence of the gospel' (Phil. 1:16). Here the emphasis falls on a positive note. The trouble which has tumbled over Paul like a deluge of rain is not pointless. It is designed to make the gospel more credible, and this has worked. Even Roman soldiers have surrendered to the Saviour (Phil. 1:13).

The gospel is well worth standing up for. During the past forty years we have seen totalitarian governments tie up dozens of nations in every area of the world. In Latin America peasants pushed out dictators and another sort of slave-master rushed in. As Africans threw off colonial control, they were quickly captured for other imperialists with a godless ideology. When China emerged from the Middle Ages into the twentieth century a band of bandits was waiting to take control. Now in all of these areas courageous Christians have stood against the forces of oppression. One thinks of Archbishop Luwum in Uganda and Watchman Nee in China. These paid in blood for their stand, but they stood until the oppressors cut them down. This is a true and worthy defence of the gospel.

With apology

Like defence, the word 'apology' is loaded with guilt. We make apologies when we have 'left undone what we should have done or do what we should not have done'. This is the gist of the prayer of general confession, as it is found in the Prayer Book.

In Bible times 'apology' had a legal meaning. It was the planned defence of an accused man or woman. We see this aspect in the modern study of apologetics, which presents reasonable arguments for Christian truth.

An apology or defence is first a *speech*. Paul introduced his speech at Jerusalem with this phrase: 'Brothers and fathers, listen now to my defence' (Acts 22:1). When forced to defend his apostleship Paul again takes the phrase: 'This is my defence to those who sit in judgement on me' (1 Cor. 9:3). In each case it was a well-reasoned rehearsal of the basis of Paul's action in proclaiming the lordship of Christ. When I was in school we were sometimes required to perform with the school band on Sunday. Each time I entered with trembling knees into the office of the Draconian director to 'make my defence' and declare why I as a Christian had a higher commitment on Sunday. That is the idea we have here, of a speech in defence of Christian communication or commitment.

The second use of our word is an *action*. Paul was summoned to a legal event, the royal visit of King Agrippa and Queen Bernice. This action was in itself a defence (Acts 25:16). Later on he experienced the same scene on a higher level when he appeared before Nero (2 Tim. 4:16). The action of appearing was in itself a defence. When someone appears in defence he may win on a technicality, when the police do not adequately warn the alleged villain. On the other hand, there may be victory on the basis of insanity, like that of Michael Fagan, who made an early morning visit to the Queen's bedroom in 1982. A third basis of victory may be the sheer weight of argument. In the end the apostle Paul lost the court case and his defence was disallowed, but he won an eternal crown (2 Tim. 4:6—8).

In the Bible 'defence', or *apologia,* has a further meaning. It expresses *evangelism.* The apostle Peter charged his contemporaries: 'Always be prepared to give an answer [*apologia*] to everyone who asks you to give a reason for the hope that you have' (1 Peter 3:15). Evangelism is seen as a reasoning explanation of the gospel.

When our son launched upon a degree course near our home, he went out one evening to a party at the college. My old parson's heart pounded a bit as I remembered the availability of drink and drugs. The next day he explained what happened. For the entire evening he had debated with a totally secular student about the reality of the Redeemer. At the end a large crowd of students had abandoned the rather pathetic band to listen to the debate. Now that is exactly what Paul means when he speaks of a defence, an apologetic, for the gospel.

Our life is a live defence for the deity of Christ. Our words are a verbal apologetic for the living Word. Our actions attract a hopeless world to the Hope of the world and a shaken society to the unshakeable Saviour.

4.
Songs of praise

'To the glory and **praise** *of God'* (Phil. 1:11)

Tourists in America are variously impressed or depressed by the quality of religious television broadcasting. One of the more financially successful electronic churches is called the 'P.T.L. Club'. The initials stand for 'Praise the Lord'. The gimmick may be a little foreign, but the idea is spot on.

When I was a lad we sang many songs almost to the point of hypnosis. One of the most frequent choices had a simple lyric:

Praise ye the Lord, Hallelujah!

That is all there was to it, and actually it was repetitious. As we know, 'Praise the Lord' translated into everyday Hebrew is 'Hallelujah'.

It is the word 'praise' that we here consider. The Greek word is *epainos*; there are few English reflections of this. It was used to praise notable men — or not to praise them, as in the low-key funeral oration: 'I come to bury Caesar, not to praise him.' The word *epainos* also was used for praise of God. The Psalms are nothing less than an ancient collection of 'Songs of Praise', a title captured by the B.B.C. for its Sunday sing-along.

The word 'praise' pops up twice in Philippians. Paul prays that the Philippians will live 'to the glory and praise of God' (Phil. 1:11). The lives of believers are designed to display the *praise of God*. Wherever they go, their presence praises the Lord. The knock-on effect is the arousing of praise in others. When people see our good works, they praise our good God (Matt. 5:16). It is like the lantern parades our children enjoyed in Germany. Each autumn nursery schools staged a candle procession. It was a sort of movable bonfire night, which marched through the village. Each child clutched a candle-lit lantern on a stick, and they sang a lovely little ditty: *Ich gehe mit meiner Laterne und meine Laterne mit mir'* ('I'm going with my lantern, and my lantern goes with me'). Proud parents lined the curb to see their little lights process past. Success was when the lantern stayed lit all evening. Christians are a massive lantern parade, and they shed light to the praise of their God.

The second use of our word in Philippians is praise for *virtues*. Paul concludes his letter by urging the Philippians: 'Whatever is true, whatever is noble, whatever is right, whatever is pure, whatever is lovely, whatever is admirable — if anything is excellent or praiseworthy — think about such things' (Phil. 4:8). This is really the Pauline power of positive thinking, and it is enforced by the inspiration of the Holy Spirit. Most Christians largely ignore this list of virtues, and as a result they are robbed of the fruit of righteousness.

Our world seems to have turned Paul's priorities upside down. In our day we are experiencing an entertainment revolution. Not only are we to be exposed to a multiplicity of television channels, but video porn shops spring up on many street corners. Many cheap cassettes deserve their nickname as 'video nasties'. Unbridled sexual bestiality is shown in explicit detail. Other nauseating nasties show sick sensation, like the one which portrayed the post-mortem on Elvis Presley. The Scripture focuses praise where it belongs. It is reserved for God in all his glory, and it is directed secondarily at people and principles which reflect divine holiness. These are worthy of praise!

Praise — where God lives

We were motoring north along the motorway one Saturday evening. Idly we scanned the dial for an interesting radio programme, but unfortunately we only found country and western music. The singer was a leather-lunged American contralto. When she came to the end of her show she introduced the obligatory hymn, and I winced. However, the

Songs of praise

explanation offered was unexpectedly perceptive. 'I thought that a hymn was a good luck charm to wind up my show,' the singer drawled. 'When success followed I fastened on the idea and always used a hymn. But I was wrong. It's not a good luck charm. The Bible sorted out my sentimental soppiness.'

By this time I was all ears, and the concluding phrase really reached my theological nerve endings. 'It's not good luck I'm interested in,' drawled the nasal nanny, 'but it's God's praise. And the Bible says, "God inhabits the praise of his people"' (AV, Psalm 22:3 actually refers to Israel).

Well, the lady's music did not do much for me, but her motives echoed some refreshing biblical thinking. The first object of praise is *God*. Predictably the Psalms are full of praise. When we married, my wife and I claimed a praise verse as our motto: 'Glorify the Lord with me; let us exalt his name together' (Ps. 34:3). It is a great verse, and pursuing it has given us a great life together.

In the New Testament Ephesians echoes the same theme. God chose us 'to the praise of his glorious grace' (Eph. 1:6). Our hope is fastened on Christ and this too achieves 'the praise of his glory' (Eph. 1:12). The same chapter assures us that our entrance into the heavenly inheritance will also present 'praise of his glory' (Eph. 1:14).

The Oxford Movement leader John Henry Newman (1801–90) left Anglicanism for Catholicism and was rewarded with a cardinal's cap. His behaviour certainly causes us as evangelical Christians to raise an eyebrow, but his praise of God is unassailable. We recall his glorious hymn:

> Praise to the Holiest in the height,
> And in the depth be praise;
> In all his words most wonderful,
> Most sure in all his ways.

There is a second object of praise, and this is worthy *men*. Pharisees made the fatal mistake of loving 'the praise of men more than praise from God' (John 12:43). True spirituality earns for people praise 'not from men, but from God' (Rom.

2:29). Good government 'commends [praises] those who do right' (1 Peter 2:14). Paul commended to Corinthian Christians a certain unnamed brother, 'who is praised by all the churches for his service to the gospel' (2 Cor. 8:18). So praise is usually earned, and it is earned by right living in God's eyes.

Praiseworthy action is seen on a national scale. As I write we have been viewing Falkland veterans on parade through the city of London. Only days before medals and honours were conferred on 800 of them. Many earned this praise at the expense of wounds, lost limbs and even lost life. Rudyard Kipling caught the flavour of fame when he wrote in *Stalky & Co.* 'A School Song':

> Let us now praise famous men —
>   Men of little showing —
> For their work continueth,
> And their work continueth,
> Broad and deep continueth,
>   Greater than their knowing.

For our purposes, however, praise is not simply a medal around the neck of someone who risked his neck. Praise is linked by the Bible to God, and praiseworthy activities are only of value because they point praise heavenwards.

Ambrose (about 339–397), the fourth-century church father, is supposed to have appended this phrase to all his work: '*Te Deum laudamus*' (We praise Thee, O God). If we live praising, we shall also speak praise and spread praise. And that is the chief end of man.

5.
Chain reaction

> *'I am in* **chains** *for Christ'* (Phil. 1:13)
> *'Because of my* **chains'** (Phil. 1:14)

Around the neck of most mayors in England hangs a chain. It is a mark of honour, and it indicates their exalted, if not powerful, political position. The luxurious car and entourage serve to undergird this impression. But the chain is the real insignia of importance.

At the other end of the social scale is another class of people. They go around in chains, too, but this is a mark of humiliation. One recalls John De Lorean, the American automotive genius who hatched the gull-winged, stainless steel sports car. After a stormy passage through the recession of the early eighties, De Lorean's dream ended up in the hands of receivers, and he ended up in the hands of the police. Television news coverage showed the pathetic picture of the erstwhile millionaire being hustled into court in handcuffs, his hands chained behind him.

Paul could have identified with the treatment of criminals, but his only crime was proclaiming liberation for slaves through Christ. Nevertheless, Paul ended up in chains, and his prison letters are full of the sound of rattling iron.

Our Greek word for 'chains' is *desmos*. It has few English relatives, but in Greek it is a colourful concept. The verb *desmeuo* meant to 'tie up in bundles', and the noun *desmios* predictably referred to prisoners, to someone who is 'tied up like a bundle'. There is a marvellous word *desmophulax* which combines *desmos* (chain) and *phulax* (to keep) in the word for a 'jailer', one who keeps people in chains. However, our attention falls on the simple word for 'chain'.

Earlier on in Philippians Paul thanks the Lord for his

Christian friends, who are in his heart: 'Whether I am in chains or defending and confirming the gospel, all of you share in God's grace with me' (Phil. 1:7). The antagonism faced by the apostle only draws Christian comforters around him. Remember the case of Georgi Vins, who suffered in Soviet Siberia before being exiled to America. I have been rereading the letters his mother Lidia wrote as she petitioned Amnesty International and the World Council of Churches on behalf of her son. Chains fasten family and friends closer together.

The second reference to chains is Paul's assertion that the gospel has been advanced through the chains he wears (Phil. 1:12,13). Although the Romans stopped the apostle, they were unable to slow down the gospel advance. In fact when Paul was imprisoned preachers of the gospel were multiplied. Prison can be turned to privilege when God is in it. Some years ago Rita Nightingale, a Lancashire lassie, was arrested in Thailand and charged. She ended up in a nightmare prison, but it also brought her into contact with a British missionary. The result was conversion, and since her release Rita Nightingale has been energetic in evangelism.

A further fruit of chains is seen in Philippians. 'Because of my chains,' Paul writes almost in amazement, 'most of the brothers in the Lord have been encouraged to speak the word of God more courageously and fearlessly' (Phil. 1:14). In other words, our suffering strengthens other saints. When Roman Christians saw how Paul was persecuted, they were liberated to spread salvation's story. In addition to my pastoral duties, I have helped out as visiting lecturer at an Anglican theological college. One of my students is a Ugandan assistant bishop, and another is a clergyman from his diocese. They told of the butchery of Idi Amin's last days. Most notable was the slaughter of Archbishop Luwum, a man of true faith. What was the result? Instead of retreating into silence, the Christians caught fresh courage and stood for God. Chains are a weak weapon against Christian courage.

Chain reaction

Prisoner's liberation

Part of my pastoral patch is Bristol's Horfield Prison, and I often either visit or preach there. Whenever I meet truly converted inmates, I am amazed at their liberation. They are free from defensiveness, because they know their sin is finally dealt with by Christ. They are free from anxiety, because they know their future is in his hands.

Our word 'chain', *desmos*, has two meanings in the Bible. First it is the *iron chain* that bound a prisoner. The demon-possessed man in Gerasene country was 'chained hand and foot and kept under guard' (Luke 8:29). Then Jesus came and snapped the links. At Philippi Paul and Silas were thrown into the 'slammer' and chained firmly, but God broke those chains too (Acts 16:26). Surely no Philippian could forget that earthquake which shocked the local church into existence. When Paul penned his letter to the Colossians he added his customary conclusion: 'I, Paul, write this greeting in my own hand,' and then he added, 'Remember my chains' (Col. 4:18). Even now we can see in our mind's eye a frail fellow struggling to handle a pen with both hands chained.

In our day we have many reminders of persecution for God's sake. The courageous Romanian Christian Josef Ton has visited many churches in Britain and his story of perseverance under pressure and prison fires all of us with added inspiration.

There is a second meaning of 'chain' in the Bible. This refers to *physical illness* as bondage. In describing the freeing of a deaf and dumb man, the Lord used picturesque language. 'The man's ears were opened', according to Mark's Gospel, 'and' (literally) 'the chain of his tongue was loosened' (Mark 7:35). Another similar statement is in the writing of Dr Luke. Again a literal translation is helpful, for Jesus argues in favour of freeing a crippled woman on the sabbath. 'Then should not this woman, a daughter of Abraham, whom Satan has kept bound for eighteen long years, be set free on the Sabbath day from what bound her' (literally 'the chain') (Luke 13:16). Here is Jesus setting prisoners free.

Chronic illness is often a chain. One recalls George Matheson (1842–1906), the blind Scottish divine who was freed from his fetter by the Lord. His eyes were blind but his spiritual vision was clear. In celebration of God's deliverance he wrote the great hymns, 'O Love that wilt not let me go' and 'Make me a captive, Lord'. Spiritual freedom far outweighed physical bondage for George Matheson.

Whether one is bound hand and foot by anti-Christian torturers, or whether one is bound by physical bonds such as blindness, true liberty is still found in Christ's hands. Charles Wesley (1707–88) sang it when he wrote,

> My chains fell off, my heart was free;
> I rose, went forth, and followed Thee.

This great Wesleyan masterpiece simply echoes the refrain of Paul. When his end drew near he gathered up his spiritual courage and wrote to young Timothy. For the young preacher's encouragement and ours Paul wrote, 'I am suffering even to the point of being chained like a criminal. But God's word is not chained' (2 Tim. 2:9).

6.
Preaching power

'Some preach *Christ out of envy and rivalry,
but others out of good will'* (Phil. 1:15)

During student days I assisted in a church composed completely of black worshippers. In this unusual setting I preached my first sermons to the accompaniment of loud shouts of approval. (At least, I thought they approved!) No sooner had I launched into my tentative introduction, than one rather robust lady let rip. 'Preach it, brother!' she screamed, 'Preach it!' When I recovered my composure I pressed on in preaching. Sometimes I miss that exuberant support.

Our word for consideration is *kerusso* (I preach). It is reflected in the technical theological word *kerygma,* which means 'the proclamation of religious truth, especially the Christian gospel'. There is a second word used in this passage, and it is *katagello* and is also translated 'to preach' (Phil. 1:17,18). However, it is the basic word of *kerusso* that we shall here examine.

No earthly occupation is so compelling as communicating the counsels of God. In our text Paul debates the motives, but he never questions the importance of preaching the gospel. In fact, he sets up preaching as a sole priority, regardless of motives (Phil. 1:18). J. D. Jones (1865–1942), the great pulpit voice of Richmond Hill Congregational Church, Bournemouth, was asked to stand for Parliament. His answer was a classic. It would have been a 'come-down', the preacher insisted, to forsake the pulpit for the political arena. Robert Murray M'Cheyne (1813–1843) lived only three decades, but he put the torch of God's glory to Scotland. When one reads Andrew Bonar's quaintly titled *Memoir and Remains* of Robert Murray M'Cheyne, there is an impressive emphasis on the power of the pulpit. M'Cheyne fully identified himself with Philip Henry's axiom: 'I would beg all the week in order to be allowed to preach on the Sabbath Day.' Preaching overpowers Paul's thinking in Philippians 1:15—18. Even though Christ be proclaimed on the faulty foundation of selfish ambition, some will hear and believe to salvation (Phil. 1:17). Dr Lloyd-Jones recounts having heard a famous sermon in the United States. In the Doctor's ears it sounded like a speech without spirit. But God still uses the Word, even when it is delivered by unworthy men in unimpressive words.

In fact, as Paul reached the climax of this little discourse on preaching, he concluded, 'Whether from false motives or true, Christ is preached. And because of this I rejoice' (Phil. 1:18). A. T. Robertson (1863—1934), who opened the Greek New Testament to generations of students at Louisville Theological Seminary, commented on this text from Philippians. 'Some Christ', claimed the professor, 'is better than no Christ at all.' Preaching may be pitiful in form, devoid of flair and feeble in faith, but it is still God's vehicle for eternal truth. And Paul put it perfectly when he wrote, 'God was pleased through the foolishness of what was preached to save those who believe' (1 Cor. 1:21).

Preaching machine

When some men meet, they discuss soccer. Every time preachers congregate, their conversation converges on other preachers and their churches. Once we were discussing a well-known English evangelist. 'He's a preaching machine,' commented my companion. What did he mean? The fellow at the focal point of our discussion is first and foremost a preacher, and his sermons have thrilled many of us.

Our word *kerusso* has three main meanings. First it is a *proclamation*. In typically apocalyptic tones, the apostle John recorded his vision: 'I saw a mighty angel proclaiming in a loud voice' (Rev. 5:2). The emphasis here is on heraldic

Preaching power

proclamation, the declaration of a message. In its original form this refers to the king's herald, an ancient version of the television party political broadcast. The emphasis was placed on a message which the monarch meant to be spread far and wide. It would be like the town crier shouting, 'Oyez, oyez, oyez!' Then that clanging bell shatters our ear drums. This proclamation conveys a message which may or may not be religious.

But the second use of our word is *prophecy*. When Jonah journeyed to Nineveh, the congenitally corrupt city repented at Jonah's preaching proclamation (Matt. 12:41). Despite his activity as ark builder and zoo collector, Noah is described in the New Testament as 'a preacher of righteousness' (2 Peter 2:5). When it came to prophetic proclamation, God gave his extraordinary message to very ordinary men. There was Elijah, the fire-eater who was prone to depression. And Jonah is synonymous with disaster, but God used him to turn back a whole city. In the New Testament we meet John the Baptist who had a very strange life-style and a tendency to doubt. Nonetheless God gathered these and many others as a corps of communicators.

There is a third meaning to our word. It is the most pertinent application to *preaching*. In the late days of Christ's ministry on earth, he urged his men: 'Preach the good news to all creation' (Mark 16:15). When faced with very refined Greeks, Paul postulated, 'God was pleased through the foolishness of what was preached to save those who believe' (1 Cor. 1:21). Even in the final days of Paul's life, he could write to Timothy, 'The Lord stood at my side and gave me strength, so that through me the message might be fully proclaimed and all the Gentiles might hear it' (2 Tim. 4:17). No human activity is any more absorbing than the preaching of the Word. In one of our family albums is a series of photographs. They are the men who have shaped my preaching. One contributed the concept of expository explanation. Another added the aspect of application, to make eternal truth relevant in time and space. There is a third, whose fine polishing of the preacher's art has infected me with a vision for pulpit perfection. Of course, these men have simply been God's instruments to hone the gift he has given.

What does the Lord's Day mean to you? It may signal a meeting with dear friends and a chance to chat after worship. To others it is a busy day of service, collecting and teaching children the Word of God. Still others must view Sunday with sadness, because they have been bound by illness and restrained from the Lord's house. To me Sunday is a gilt-edged day when I have the privilege of preaching God's revelation to God's people in God's house.

7.
Dead end

'Whether by life or by **death'** (Phil. 1:20)

Few words in English are so colourfully employed as 'death' or 'dead'. To 'flog a dead horse' means persisting in a project or subject which has no more life in it. A 'dead end street' is the American equivalent of the English (and French) cul-de-sac. When a parishioner is 'dead to the world', he is also beyond hearing any sermon. A 'dead language' is learned by pupils in pain. And a 'dead lock' assures that the house is secure from intruders, at least through the door.

Put it all together, and 'death' means the absence of life, movement, perception. Finally, of course, each person passes into the realm of the dead, and all relationships and responsibilities in this world are broken off, although the Christian is convinced that reality reaches beyond the barrier of death.

The Greek word for death is *thanatos,* and it is reflected in English. For instance, recently there has been a resurgence of interest in 'thanatology', the science of death. In some secondary schools there is even a course of study which delves into the depths of death, describing the physical, pyschological and social implications of death. It is a rather morbid exercise, especially when Christianity is not allowed to explain death.

Death to the apostle Paul was not an enemy but an ally. He saw death as a vehicle to *glorify Christ.* 'As always Christ will be exalted in my body,' Paul insisted, 'whether by life or by death' (Phil. 1:20). He followed through on that principle by proclaiming that for him 'to live is Christ and to die is gain' (Phil. 1:21). Surely this verse is the single most profound philosophy of life ever stated. The unique nature of this statement can be seen by comparison. Try filling in the blanks: 'For me to live is . . . , to die is . . .' For me to live is *money*, to die is *to leave it all*. (One recalls the pathetic picture of Howard Hughes, the animal-like tycoon who died rich but ruined.) For me to live is *fame*, to die is to be *forgotten*. (The silver screen of the cinema world is littered with little-remembered stars who lost their twinkle.) Paul's passion for Christ was the life of his living and the light of his dying.

A second aspect of death is the *death of Christ*. In his incarnation Christ 'became obedient to death — even death on a cross' (Phil. 2:8). Death for Christ was the unavoidable will of God the Father. To effect the atonement, there must be the sacrifice of a lamb. In Christ's crucifixion all the sacrificial system of Judaism was fulfilled to God's glory and our eternal good. The nineteenth-century critic David Friedrich Strauss (1808—74) propounded the preposterous theory that Christ had not died on the cross. He had only swooned, fainted and the cool of the tomb revived him. This cut the very nerve-ending of biblical atonement, for the sacrifice had to die a real death, and this Christ did on behalf of his people.

In the Philippian letter Paul presents Epaphroditus, the Philippian emissary, who was *near death*. Twice Paul emphasizes it: 'He was ill, and almost died' (Phil. 2:27); 'He almost died for the work of Christ' (Phil. 2:30). This fact elevated Epaphroditus to the front rank of gospel advance, and Paul praised God for the courage of that Philippian brother. Since then many have come near to death. Our dear Professor V. Raymond Edman (1900—67) hovered at death's door in an Ecuadorian hut, as he watched his wife dye her wedding dress black for the funeral. But God spared him a further forty years to teach successive generations of Wheaton College students the lessons of living for God.

One final occurrence of our word, *death*, is found in Philippians. It is the *death of devotion*. Christians become participants in the very death of Christ. They become 'like him in his death' (Phil. 3:10). Paul portrays a total identification of the Christian with Christ in resurrection power,

Dead end

which energizes our spiritual lives. There is also a oneness with Christ's sufferings, which gives boldness to face difficulty. Finally we plunge to the depths of death, surrendering all personal prerogatives to his lordship.

Death in Philippians, and indeed in all New Testament thought, is not only an enemy. It is the ally of every Christian in living to God's glory.

Death and taxes

The wise old philosopher, statesman Benjamin Franklin (1706-90) is credited with the statement: 'There is nothing so certain as death and taxes.' Well, if he could say that in revolutionary America, what would he have said in our world of income, property, value added and excise taxes? This would have taxed his vocabulary even more. The nature and scope of taxation may have changed over the past two centuries, but death still has the same nature and scope. Death carries away every person sooner or later, and its nature is still a radical break with life on this earth.

Death applies first of all to *nature*. Jesus did not avoid the reality of death and stated it rather bluntly. When the disciples did not understand the facts about Lazarus, Jesus said, 'Lazarus is dead' (John 11:14); even death would demonstrate God's glory.

The significance of natural death was formulated clearly by the writer of Hebrews. 'Just as man is destined to die once', he wrote, 'and after that to face judgement' (Heb. 9:27). This rather direct description of death is sobering. I shall never forget the look on the faces of a congregation of motor-cycle jockeys, when I took this text for my address at the funeral of one of their friends.

Another New Testament reference to death is the *death of Christ*. Most New Testament books refer to this momentous event. We who once were 'God's enemies . . . were reconciled to him' through Christ's death (Rom. 5:10). 'It was impossible for death to keep its hold on him [Christ]', according to Peter at Pentecost (Acts 2:24). Each time we gather at the Lord's Table, we 'proclaim the Lord's death until he comes' (1 Cor. 11:26). Recently a young preacher visited our city. One evening he described in well-researched detail the death of Christ. God so empowered that statement of Christ's passion, that at least one young woman was drawn to saving grace by it. She later could recount every detail of Christ's death for her, and her life now bears the marks of it.

The New Testament also speaks of *spiritual death*. 'If a man keeps my word,' Jesus said, 'he will never see death' (John 8:51). When Christ came he was a light dawning upon 'those living in the land of the shadow of death' (Matt. 4:16). According to John's first letter, 'We know that we have passed from death to life, because we love our brothers' (1 John 3:14). Spiritual death is being cut off from God by our sin and trespasses. Christ reverses this rigor mortis when he touches us with his salvation. It is like a telephone which is 'dead'. You can dial all you wish, but a fault in the line makes the instrument quite useless. Only when the connection to the exchange has been established does the line become live and communication possible. Christ establishes communication between sinful people and a holy God.

There is a final death in the Bible. It is *eternal death*. Paul describes non-Christians as 'slaves to sin, which leads to death' (Rom. 6:16). Jesus Christ 'destroyed (eternal) death and . . . brought life and immortality to light through the gospel' (2 Tim. 1:10). Eternal death is not only hell fire. Neither is it simply submission to Satan's control for ever. Nor is it only the torture of hell. Eternal death is first and foremost being cut off from God for ever. Since God is the sole source of life from creation to consummation of history, to be separated from him is eternal death. The only cure for that is the Lord who gives eternal life.

8.
Fresh fruit

'This will mean **fruitful** *labour for me'* (Phil. 1:22)

Fruit usually appeals to our tastebuds. In fact, our lives have been spiced by certain fruits. When I was a boy back in Michigan there were hot summers with stacks of strawberries and ice cream. Even now the taste comes back in a wave of sweet memory. While we were raising our young children in Germany there were other fruits. Oranges were a treat which the children loved. Most nights they would nibble apples in their beds, concealing the cores for discovery by mum when she tidied up their rooms. Now we are enjoying other fruits. West Indian members of our fellowship keep us supplied with such exotic specialities as mangoes, pineapples and even plantain. (Plantain is a banana-like fruit and a tasty dish fried or raw.)

But the apostle Paul does not refer to edible fruit in Philippians. He is hungry for spiritual fruit. The Greek word for fruit is *karpos,* and in the Scriptures it is applied both to physical and spiritual fruits. The word occurs sixty-six times in the New Testament, and a brief consideration of it will be most 'fruitful'.

Three times in Philippians Paul speaks of 'fruit', and on each occasion he gives the word a special twist. Fruit to Paul is the *product of righteous living.* For Philippian Christians Paul prays that they may be 'filled with the fruit of righteousness that comes through Jesus Christ — to the glory and praise of God' (Phil. 1:11). As Christ imputes righteousness to Christians this total transformation sprouts out in right behaviour, 'fruit of righteousness'. Recently a middle-aged couple were soundly saved in our fellowship. In the subsequent months their thought patterns, actions and even appetites have been turned over. Almost weekly some new 'fruit of righteousness' flourishes in their lives.

A second crop of spiritual fruit is seen also in Philippians. Paul desires prolonged life only because 'this will mean fruitful labour' (Phil. 1:22). Many times we place a high priority on faithfulness, and this is right. But the New Testament places an even higher priority on *fruitfulness*. Paul was not just marking time or treading water, as he endured Roman arrest. Far more, he was planning to produce a harvest of heavenly fruit through his endeavours.

A particularly powerful example of fruitfulness in pastoral ministries was Robert Murray M'Cheyne, whom I mentioned in a previous chapter. During the Dundee revival M'Cheyne calculated that upwards of 800 people 'conversed with different ministers in apparent anxiety'. Not all were truly converted, according to M'Cheyne, but some did believe to salvation. 'President Jonathan Edwards considered it likely', according to the Scottish preacher, 'that . . . the proportion of real conversions might resemble the proportion of blossoms in the spring and fruit in the autumn.'[1] Not all fruit came to fruition, but some fruit was surely harvested both in the colonial Great Awakening and the Dundee revival.

A final reference to fruit applies to the Philippian Christians. Paul thanked them for their practical care of him, and then he added, 'I desire fruit that may abound to your account' (Phil. 4:17, AV). When the Christians contributed to sustain their imprisoned brother Paul, *God rewarded them with fruit*. It is a continual source of amazement to me that Christians do not grasp this elementary spiritual principle: 'You cannot out-give the Lord.' A retired minister recently shared with me how God has provided for him and his wife. He was animated and astonished, but I recalled the sacrificial financial giving which accompanied his blessed pastoral ministry. He gave back to the church much of his small salary, and God has repaid this investment with handsome dividends.

The obvious implication of this little survey of the word 'fruit' in Philippians is this: God is the source of all spiritual fruit. When our lives glorify God, it is the fruit of his righteousness at work in us. When our ministries flourish, it is God who makes us fruitful. When money stretches to meet need, it is the fruit of God's good provision. So every day is a harvest thanksgiving for the Christian.

God's fruit inspection

The problem with fruit is the waiting. Some years ago we stuck an apple tree in the ground in front of our house. Then we waited for several years and we nursed it through the drought of 1976. All to no avail, for fruit never appeared. When we sold the house, I was glad to pass on the appleless tree. By contrast we planted another apple tree soon after settling in our Bristol manse. Two years later we had a remarkable apple crop, which I snacked on during the walk from our garage to the kitchen door. Crisp, crunchy and juicy, the apples are a delicious fruit.

In the New Testament the word *karpos* is used in three ways. First it stands for *edible fruit*. Jesus spoke in an axiom when he said, 'Make a tree good and its fruit will be good, or make a tree bad and its fruit will be bad' (Matt. 12:33). The parable of the sower and the seed centres around the fruitfulness of seed sown, and the good ground brought forth fruit ('a crop') a hundred times as large as the seed (Matt. 13:8). When Elijah prayed, the rain came and the earth brought forth fruit (James 5:18). It is good to remember that fruit is from God. Although a harvest display is a relic of bygone days when most people had a garden, it does remind us of the fruitfulness God gives. One year I showed the children small seeds and explained that fruit and vegetables grew from such small seeds. To my amazement, most of the big city children at our church *did* recognize the seed and the fruit.

There is a second use of the word *karpos* (fruit) in the New Testament. This is the fruit of human reproduction, *children*. Jesus is described before his birth as 'the fruit of Mary's womb' (Luke 1:42 AV). David's descendants are likewise known as 'the fruit of his loins' (Acts 2:30, AV). In the New International Version, these rather explicit pictures are toned down to read: 'Blessed is the child you will bear' (Luke 1:42) and 'God . . . would place one of his (David's) descendants on his throne' (Acts 2:30). Children are still a beautiful fruit of marriage, especially when it is a Christian marriage. Sometimes the little one comes along after many years of marriage, and at other times the baby is born when parents are past the normal child-bearing years. However, whenever God gives a lovely, healthy little one, it is the fruit of his blessing.

Finally fruit is *spiritual*. Jesus told his disciples: 'This is to my Father's glory, that you bear much fruit' (John 15:8). In the same discourse the Lord said, 'You did not choose me, but I chose you to go and bear fruit — fruit that will last' (John 15:16). In writing to the Galatians, Paul enumerates the fruit of the Spirit, which characterizes Christian living (Gal. 5:22). Recently a man professed faith in Christ and repentance of past sin. For him repentance was costly because he had broken the law and landed in prison. After release he has shown some signs of true repentance and new life. These are a welcome harvest of spiritual fruit.

Fruit can be encouraged. In nature we fertilize, and in the spiritual realm we edify and encourage. But in the final analysis fruit springs from God's grace, and this is true whether it is cumquats or Christian character.

1. A. Bonar, *Memoir and Remains of R. M'Cheyne*, p. 121.

9.
Agony and ecstasy

'Contending *as one man for the faith of the gospel*' (Phil. 1:27)
'*The same* **struggle** *you saw I had*' (Phil. 1:30)

The Agony and the Ecstasy was Irving Stone's caption over the life of Buonarroti Michelangelo (1475–1564), the Renaissance sculptor, painter and poet. Actually Stone's book, which was turned into a film, portrays the most extensive project in the artist's life, the painting of the ceiling in the Vatican's Sistine Chapel. More than a decade was needed to paint frescoes on 10,000 square feet of ceiling, and the paintings portray a panorama of biblical history spanning everything from creation to the Last Judgement. More than four centuries have slipped by since Michelangelo put down his paints, but the Sistine Chapel is still a star attraction for tourists to Rome. Michelangelo's agony left a legacy of ecstasy for successive generations.

But it is the agony that Paul presents in Philippians. In fact, the Greek word he uses is *agon* or *agonizomai* (ancestor of the English word 'agonize'). In Greek the word referred to an athletic contest, a struggle or a fight. A similar word is *athleo*, from which our word 'athlete' comes. This term tells the story of an organized contest or competition contained by rules. In any case, both words suggest a struggle or strife.

Paul defines life in a 'manner worthy of the gospel of Christ' by saying it means 'standing firm in one spirit, contending as one man for the faith of the gospel' (Phil. 1:27). Here we have that 'athletic' word *athleo* wedded to a prefix *sun* (together). Literally it reads 'contend together'. It is a team effort which Paul portrays here. Christians team up to defeat the forces of evil inside or outside the church. In

43

fact Paul describes the opponents as those who seek to frighten and oppose Christians (Phil. 1:28). In the face of such frightening opposition, Christians stand together as a team. The Christian life is a team event.

At the end of Philippians Paul again returns to the 'athletic' image. 'Help these women', Paul pleads, for they 'contended [*athleo*] at my side in the cause of the gospel' (Phil. 4:3). It is remarkable that a 'star combatant' like the apostle Paul places so much emphasis on the team-work of Christian living. The point of our first word, *sunathleo*, is clear: the spiritual struggle is not won by outstanding individual effort. It is a contest where contenders compete in teams. God's team is his church.

The second word for struggle in Philippians is *agon*, the ancestor of our word 'agony'. Here the focus falls not on the contest, but on the contestant. The cost of spiritual success is 'agony' or 'struggle'. As the apostle put it, 'You are going through the same struggle you saw I had' (Phil. 1:30). They had viewed his beating and imprisonment. His humiliation was fresh in their memories, despite a decade of past history. Still they recalled the sight of bleeding backs and bound hands and feet. And the strong song of victory which rang out from the Philippian jail still sounded in their ears. They were aware of the spiritual struggle.

Needless to say, first-century Christians had many disadvantages. Their faith was beset by detractors. Their fellowship was frequently thinned by persecution. They did not even have a written revelation, other than apostolic epistles. The government frowned on their worship, relegating them to the lunatic fringe of ancient civilization. But one thing they did know: they knew that discipleship with a suffering Christ and support of persecuted leaders gave them courage to contend for the gospel. And in conflict they were courageous.

In his famous Hibbert Lectures (published 1888), the persuasive Professor Edwin Hatch (1835–89) summed up the Christian life in this phrase: 'Life is in reality an Olympic festival: we are God's athletes to whom he has given an opportunity of showing of what stuff we are made.'

Agony and ecstasy

Fight the good fight

Some battles are worth fighting. When a patient persists in the battle against disease, he or she actually feels better. Disease may defeat him in the end, but the battle has been worthwhile. Another fight worth the trouble is the struggle against violence. In the big cities there is a rising tide of tumult and street crime. Still many Christians are contending alongside civic and police officials against the flood. They may not be winning, but they are slowing it down. It is also worth fighting against the secular drift in education. There is a prevailing philosophy which says man sprang from an accidental collision of molecules, that he lives as a puppet of social circumstances and that death is the door into a vast, empty void. Many Christian professors, parents and pastors are standing up against this system of thought, and it is a battle worth engaging in.

Paul urged Christians to compete as *athletes*. To young Timothy Paul wrote, 'If anyone competes as an athlete [*athle*], he does not receive the victor's crown unless he competes according to the rules' (2 Tim. 2:5). The Hebrew Christians were also commended, because they 'stood [their] ground in a great contest [*athlesis*], in the face of suffering' (Heb. 10:32). Contests are costly. It is one thing to hook, jab and slug a punching bag in the gymnasium. When the opponent strikes back with equal or greater force, it is a far more painful contest. We can dream dreams about spiritual living, but the daily battle with our adversary in all his forms is a contest more demanding than any athletic event.

Paul also used the second word for struggle. It is our word *agon* or *agony*. First it refers to encounter. In his final paragraph Paul claimed, 'I have fought the good fight', literally 'I have agonized a good agony' (2 Tim. 4:7). The writer of Hebrews put it in another picture: 'Run with perseverance the race marked out for us,' or literally, 'Let us run with patience the agony marked out for us' (Heb. 12:1). The point of this picture is simple. Christian living is no stroll in the park. When we first went to Germany, we learned about the Sunday afternoon stroll, the *Spaziergang*. Dressed in the best Sunday finery, the whole family would march through the forest for a couple of hours before returning home to a waist-stretching coffee table groaning under cakes and sweets. It was a lovely relaxing family custom. But the Christian life is not like a *Spaziergang*; it is rather more like a run through an obstacle course which leaves us exhausted, ruffled and sweat-soaked. This is the 'agony' of which the New Testament speaks.

There is another application of our word. It is *prayer*. In closing his Colossian letter, Paul recommends Epaphras, who was distinguished by 'always wrestling [agonizing] in prayer for you, that you may stand firm in all the will of God, mature and fully assured' (Col. 4:12). Of the Roman Christians Paul speaks similarly: 'Join me in my struggle [agony] by praying to God for me' (Rom. 15:30). One of the more neglected aspects of Christian service is prayer. Many people like to speak in public, despite the preparation required. Many enjoy singing in a large congregation. Most Christians would willingly invite a friend or witness over the garden fence. Very few will devote great blocks of time to prayer.

Dr A. W. Tozer was known mainly as a powerful preacher and writer. Few knew the secret of his power. It is Alan Redpath who told us. Dr Tozer was in the habit of going to the lake front of Chicago in the spring and summer. From early morning onwards he would spend two to three hours in prayer. Perhaps if we persisted in the agony of prayer, we would see more of the ecstasy of spiritual power.

10.
Mind set

'Make my joy complete by being like-minded' (Phil. 2:2)
'One in spirit [mind] *and purpose'* (Phil. 2:2)

Attitude is all important. Doctors tell us that patients who want to recover are more likely to make progress than those who have 'lost the will to live'. This is one reason why some people act younger at eighty than others do at seventy. In our church we have an eighty-year-old who works circles around many younger folk, and some of our senior citizens can outsmart people half their age. Attitude makes a big difference.

The same is true in spiritual matters. Paul resorts to a marvellously adaptable Greek word to describe our attitude. It is the word *phroneo*, 'to think, hold an opinion, judge, set one's mind'. It is our attitude which here comes into focus. The Greek word *phroneo* does not have connections with any English word, but it occurs in various forms about two dozen times, and almost half of these are in the short script to the Philippians.

In the passage under consideration there are two references. Philippian believers are urged to be 'like-minded', 'one in spirit and purpose' (*phronountes*) (Phil. 2:2). Christians are characterized by shared opinions. It is not a unity arising out of a common cause, like the Campaign for Nuclear Disarmament. Neither is this unity based upon membership of the same organization, as one can see by the diversity in any given political party. Christian unity is not even commitment to a common interest, like classical music, football or even bird-watching. Christian unity is really a shared attachment to the Lord. As a magnet attracts metal shavings, so the Lord draws together Spirit-controlled people.

Our word *phroneo* is also found in other spots throughout Philippians. 'It is right for me to feel [*phroneo*, think] this way about you' Paul claims, 'since I have you in my heart' (Phil. 1:7). Here emotional attachment is the meaning of our word. As a young man thinks constantly about his sweetheart, so the mind is controlled by thoughts of our spiritual loved ones.

In his great Christological passage, Paul introduces the 'attitude . . . [mind] of Christ Jesus' (Phil. 2:5). When one surrenders to the lordship of Christ, the control of the Master must be total. Even our mind must be sold out to the Lord. Like Johannes Kepler (1571–1630), the father of modern astronomy, we 'think God's thoughts after him'. Our mind is mastered by our heavenly Master.

In Paul's strong section on sanctification, he also refers to our word. 'All of us who are mature should take such a view [think the same] of things' insists the apostle, 'and if on some point you think differently, that too God will make clear to you' (Phil. 3:15). A few verses later he returns to the same subject. Enemies of the cross display depraved attitudes. 'Their mind is on earthly things' (Phil. 3:19). They think like this world thinks, and therefore they are in no way spiritual. As Christians grow towards maturity in their faith, they become more at one in their thought patterns. We are what we think.

When Paul chides two ladies, Euodia and Syntyche, about their fractured fellowship, he tells them straight out: 'Agree [think alike] with each other in the Lord' (Phil. 4:2). In fact, the Greek Testament is most economical with words at this point. 'Think the same in the Lord' is Paul's command. Most moderns bristle when they are told to 'think the same'. But this is the genius of biblical Christianity, and it is the answer to most petty peevishness in the churches.

One final reference to our word occurs in Philippians. 'I rejoice greatly in the Lord', Paul thanks them, 'that at last you have renewed your concern [thinking] for me' (Phil. 4:10). Paul was always on the Philippians' mind. Their thinking was not the lock-step mentality of young people brainwashed by cults. It was the whole-hearted agreement of Christians controlled by the Holy Spirit. Such minds are not sapped of creativity but released to be creative on God's scale.

Mind over matter

Recently a member of our congregation invited us to visit the school where he is acting headmaster. It is a rather unusual school, amply staffed and lavishly supplied by the local council. Its pupils are unusual, too. They are all handicapped. After our assembly talk, there was a time of sharing. One child could boast of a new achievement. He had stood without the aid of sticks for several minutes, a milestone achievement in his life. What an example this was of the triumph of heart over handicap! And the teacher beamed as the other pupils applauded this achievement.

The Greek word under consideration, *phroneo*, has as one of its main meanings this sort of *determination*. 'Think of others', Paul wrote to the Romans (NIV, 'Live in harmony with one another', Rom. 12:16). The determined mind-set of Christians is concern for others, and this sets them apart from the rest of the human rat race.

To Colossian Christians Paul wrote, 'Set your minds on things above, not on earthly things' (Col. 3:2). When Peter protested at the plan of Christ's crucifixion, the Lord told him: 'You do not have in mind the things of God, but the things of men' (Matt. 16:23).

Christian commitment involves certain convictions. Alternatives are ruled out from the start. Lying is not an alternative; the Christian is bound by the truth. Hatred is not in the Christian's emotional armoury; he is going to love even his enemies. Immorality is not just a harmless sexual adventure; it is a violation of basic belief. Christians have 'set their minds' on the things of God.

The second related meaning of our word is *our regular thought processes*. These arise out of the basic set of our mind. A few illustrations will show what is meant. Roman

Jews came to Paul with this request: 'We want to hear what your views [thoughts] are' (Acts 28:22).

Negatively Paul urged anti-Jewish Christians not to be 'arrogant', literally 'to think highly of themselves' (Rom. 11:20). The same use of our word is found in Paul's letter to Timothy. 'Command those who are rich in this present world', Paul advises Timothy, 'not to be arrogant [literally 'think highly'] nor to put their hope in wealth' (1 Tim. 6:17).

So our thought processes are very important. A child usually thinks the world revolves around him. Christmas proves to the childish mind a converse truth: 'It is more blessed to receive than to give.' Teenagers are dominated by the desire to assert their personalities, and this often looks like rebellion. Most men think about what polishes their image, while women are concerned about security. This over-simplification shows some of the elements which make us think as we do. It is God's goal to release us from all of these mental strait-jackets and free us to think his thoughts. It is his mind over all that matters in our lives.

11.
In form

> *'Who, being in very nature* [form] *God'* (Phil. 2:6)
> *'Taking the very nature* [form] *of a servant'* (Phil. 2:7)

'Form' for most of us conjures up pictures of size and shape. When our children were small, my wife produced birthday cakes in the form of animals, elephants, giraffes and horses. Our grandmothers used dress 'forms' to tailor home-made clothes. One remembers these headless, armless and legless torsos tucked away in the attic.

In the Bible passage mentioned above, however, 'form' is used interchangeably with 'nature' or essence. It is not just the outward appearance, but the total reality of the person. This agreement of shape and reality is seen in sport. When someone wins a tennis final, the commentator sometimes says, 'She was in winning *form* today.' Her performance matches her potential. This is the idea which dominates the use of our word in Philippians 2.

The Greek word translated variously as 'form' or 'nature' is *morphē*. One sees it in such English words as 'morphology', the study of forms of animals, plants or words. Another occurrence of the word is in 'meta*morpho*sis', changing of forms. A caterpillar turns into a butterfly, or a tadpole hops up to life as a frog.

The biblical fact that Christ exists in divine *and* human form is one of the great riddles of revelation. The scholar and bishop J. B. Lightfoot (1828–89) states the significance of *morphē* with admirable simplicity: *'Morphē* implies not the external accidents [characteristics], but the essential attributes.'[1] It is not just the outward shape but the inward reality that our word displays.

Remembering the fulness of the word, we turn to the

Philippian letter. In the first appearance we learn that Jesus was 'in very nature [or form] God' (Phil. 2:6). The outward reality was seen only by eternal beings but the inward truth of his divinity was displayed throughout the incarnation. His continuous state of being is divine, and this in no way diminishes deity. Jesus Christ is, and always has been, God. When the divine attributes shone through the human shape, it was like the sun breaking through a cloud cover. Although the clouds sometimes hide the sun from view, its fire has not gone out. So when the clouds break ever so slightly the sun streams through. Although humanness hid the divine essence from view, at times like the transfiguration Christ's essential deity dawned on the world.

A second occurrence of our word refers to Christ's humanity. The Lord in his incarnation took 'the very nature of a servant' (Phil. 2:7). This was not an exchange of the human for the divine. It was the addition of the human to the divine. In Christ eternal deity took human and humble flesh (John 1:14). The Lord's essential humility was seen in his poverty. He was born in a borrowed manger, slept in borrowed beds, preached from the pulpit of a borrowed boat and his corpse was buried in a borrowed tomb. The only Person who had any rights to assert waived his right to assert them. As Lightfoot put it, 'He who is Master of all is slave of all.' In his humiliation Christ did not divest himself of deity, but he did lay down the expression of his deity.

There is a third appearance of our word in Philippians. It is a combination word, and it crops up when Paul sets down his priorities. His aim is threefold: 'to know Christ and the power of his resurrection and the fellowship of sharing in his sufferings, becoming like [literally, 'conformed' to] him in his death' (Phil. 3:10). 'Conformity' comes from two Greek words meaning 'formed with', or fitted to a certain shape. When a sculptor forms a figure, he first shapes a mould and then pours the substance into the mould. After it sets the final figure emerges. Christians are 'conformed' to Christ. He is the mould that gives shape to their lives. Both their appearance and their essence are shaped by the Saviour. This frees them progressively from being 'conformed' to the world (Rom. 12:2).

Reformed by the Creator

Between conversion and the Christian's coronation day in glory, there is a lot to be done. The technical word is 'sanctification', making one holy. God works like a Master Sculptor, shaping the saint to make him fit for heaven. And the Lord is the Model, the form into which we are being shaped.

Our word *morphē* ('form' or 'nature') occurs only about five times in the New Testament. First it is the *resurrected form of Christ*. On the road to Emmaus 'Jesus appeared in a different form to two of them while they were walking in the country' (Mark 16:12). So different was the appearance of the resurrected Redeemer that the disciples could not discern him (Luke 24:13—35). So the matter of form is affected by resurrection. Not only does the resurrection body look different, it also has new and improved qualities of mobility. Christ passed through doors, to the shock of his scared band of followers. The form of a new body revealed the nature of a new person.

The second focus of 'form' is *the Christian*. 'For those God foreknew he also predestined to be conformed to the likeness of his Son', wrote the apostle Paul with spiritual penetration, 'that he [Christ] might be the firstborn among many brothers' (Rom. 8:29). Here is the idea of progressive sanctification, as God moulds us like little characters out of modelling clay. He shapes us inwardly and outwardly to the likeness of his Son, our Saviour. The idea here is that of an exact likeness, like twins who are indistinguishable from one another. They sound alike, look alike and even display the same reflexes and habits. God is at work to shape us in the same sort of likeness to his Son. When we see him, we shall indeed be like him (1 John 3:2).

The same idea occurs in another verse, where the apostle Paul speaks of Christians 'who with unveiled faces all reflect the Lord's glory'. Then Paul sketches the means by which we are 'conformed': we are being 'transformed into his [the Lord's] likeness with ever-increasing glory, which comes from the Lord, who is the Spirit' (2 Cor. 3:18). It is like an egg which is formed within the chicken. At a certain point it is laid and fertilized. Then the long wait ensues, with the hen poised over the egg. After the appropriate time a fuzzy little chick wiggles out of the broken egg. The fragile egg has given way to a downy little chick. However, this transformation, which always amazes little eyes, is nothing in comparison with the change going on in every Christian. He is being transformed from a fallen fragment of humanity into the soaring likeness of the glorified Saviour.

There is a final forming and it involves *Christ himself*. Paul agonizes with 'the pains of childbirth until Christ is formed in you' (Gal. 4:19). Spiritual people are persistently concerned for new Christians, that they may grow up. Here Paul envisages the final product of spiritual growth, the emergence of Christ's image in the Christian's life. It is like those sophisticated cameras which produce an undeveloped photograph as soon as the shutter is snapped. As the photographer looks on, the image emerges slowly until a fully finished colour snapshot shows up. At conversion Christ imprints our lives. In the years that follow Christ becomes increasingly formed in us.

It is a long way from Christ in the 'form of God' (Phil. 2:6) to Christ being formed in the believer. But the same divine plan which precipitated the incarnation also produces the image of Christ in us. How far has his image developed in you?

1. J. B. Lightfoot, *St Paul's Epistle to the Philippians,* p. 110.

12.
Famous names

'Gave him a **name** *that is above every* **name***'* (Phil. 2:9)
'At the **name** *of Jesus every knee should bow'* (Phil. 2:10)

'What's in a name?' Shakespeare set the question in *Romeo and Juliet*[1]. Then the Bard answered his own question: 'That which we call a rose by any other name would smell just as sweet.'

However, for a historian or a disc jockey, names are very important. Some say dismissively, 'I can remember faces, but I just can't remember names.' This is a rather superficial approach to acquaintance or friendship.

The Greek word for 'name' is *onoma* and it appears no less than 193 times in the Greek New Testament. We see shadows of this Greek word in technical terms such as 'onomatopoeia', 'names which resemble the sounds they describe'. (A couple of examples are the 'cuckoo' call, or the 'sizzle' of bacon in a pan.) There is even a faint flavour of the Greek word *onoma* in its more popular Latin equivalent *nomen*.

Our word for 'name' appears three times in Philippians. First of all, it is the 'name above every name' which God gave Jesus in glory (Phil. 2:9). There is a great debate about the exact nature of this name. Some famous commentators such as Bishop Lightfoot think it is a secret name known only to the Godhead. (It is, according to him, a name 'of Jesus', that is an additional name given to Jesus. Some even conjecture that it is the name of Jehovah.) Whatever the name is, the fact remains. Jesus Christ was honoured especially by God the Father in the resurrection and ascension. It is like the honour heaped upon a famous person, such as Field Marshal Montgomery, who later became Viscount Montgomery of Alamein.

The following verse builds upon our understanding of the name given to Jesus. When history winds up, the Official Receiver is the Lord Jesus Christ. According to the apostle, 'At the name of Jesus every knee should bow, in heaven and on earth and under the earth' (Phil. 2:10). What a picture of sovereign power this paints! In bold strokes we see the demons cowering, the angels bending, glorified saints giving glory and every living person prostrate. As they fall flat, there will be a thunderous cry: 'Jesus Christ is Lord!' And God will gather the glory to himself. A pale reflection of this was seen at the coronation of the Queen. When the crown was in place the cry filled the abbey: 'God Save The Queen!' Then the voices echoed through the stone sanctuary: 'God Save The Queen!' Television cameras flashed the glory to other continents. But the glory of our Christ will be broadcast by no man-made media but rather by the sheer swelling sound of kneeling praise. All earthly coronations will fade into a whisper by comparison.

The third reference to names is personal and pertains to Christians. They are those 'whose names are in the book of life' (Phil. 4:3). After the stratospheric statements about the name of the Lord, we now come down to earth with a bang. Paul speaks of fellow-workers. Although he has enshrined many names in the New Testament, he knows that God has an indelible and indestructible record in 'the Lamb's book of life'. Our names have a future beyond history. When we prowl through the cemeteries of our town, we notice many famous names. Some, like George Müller, are even spiritually significant, and others were important men of industry, politics and education. Those gravestones will crumble in time, but true Christians have a more permanent memorial. It is in the 'Lamb's book of life'! God has written them down, and he will never erase them.

Christian names

In our multi-racial society the concept of a Christian name has been re-evaluated. Ask a young Hindu lad about his

Famous names

'Christian name', and he will be dumbfounded. The same is true of Muslims, Buddhists and even nonconformists who have not been christened. The American custom of speaking of 'first names' and 'last names' is gathering momentum in Britain.

At any rate there are two basic applications of our concept of 'name' in the Bible. First, the word is used for *people*. In the early days of Christ's earthly ministry he selected a band of disciples; then the New Testament lists the names of the twelve (Matt. 10:2—4). Otherwise undistinguished men enter the ranks of immortality because Christ called them.

When the forerunner was born, God gave him a name. Zechariah was instructed by the angel to name the baby 'John' (Luke 1:13). Although the neighbours could not quite comprehend it, the parents put the name 'John' to their baby boy. He grew up to be the greatest prophet who ever lived (Matt. 11:9—11). Jesus said so himself.

People are important individuals in God's economy of things. There are at least three reasons for this. First, God *created* individuals, who are as distinctive as fingerprints. Second, God re-creates people when his grace restores the wrecks of humanity and puts them together again as new people. Third, everyone will share in the new creation, when God makes a whole new world to contain his race of new people.

The second application of our word 'name' is the name of the *Lord*. In Jesus' words, we gather in his name, and he gives identity to our fellowship (Matt. 18:20). Early disciples performed the most spectacular miracles, and the power source was the name of the Lord Jesus Christ (Acts 4:7,10). True spiritual liberation only flows from the name of the Lord Jesus Christ (Acts 4:12).

In the epistles the same sense of power prevails. When Christians live out the life of the Lord their aim is simple: 'that the name of the Lord Jesus Christ may be glorified in you' (2 Thess. 1:12). As the penman of Hebrews wound up his letter, he urged Christians to 'continually offer to God a sacrifice of praise — the fruit of lips that confess his name' (Heb. 13:15).

The Christian conceives of Christ as the focus of all that is meaningful. In fact, the name of the Lord becomes the centre around which everything turns and the basis upon which the entire life is built. Beyond this the Christian reveres the name of the Lord as he would a dear loved one. The name of the Lord Jesus Christ is inexpressibly precious to the true believer. For that reason any profanity of that name is unbearable, be it in the media, conversation or even thought. The Christian thus identifies with Caroline Noel (1817–77), who wrote,

> At the name of Jesus,
> Every knee shall bow,
> Every tongue confess him
> King of glory now;
> 'Tis the Father's pleasure
> We should call him Lord,
> Who from the beginning
> Was the mighty Word.

1. Act 2, Scene 2.

13.
Powerful presence

'You have always obeyed — not only in my **presence***'*
(Phil. 2:12)

When a great person is present, there is a special atmosphere. It must have been 1948. The year is shrouded in the mists of my middle-aged memory; the day is etched clearly on the photographic plate of my mind. Although my family was traditionally Republican, we all turned out to see the President, that earthy Missourian Harry Truman (1884–1972). Having been propelled into the presidency by the death of Roosevelt in 1945, the tough Truman now sought (and surprisingly won) election in his own right. As he came to woo the workers of Pontiac (Michigan), the President's presence lent lustre to our soot-stained street.

It is this idea of a powerful 'presence' that permeates our Greek word *parousia*. At a recent ministers' meeting Donald MacLeod discussed the *parousia*. Not only does *parousia* portray the coming again of Christ; there is also the idea of his illuminating, glittering, glorious presence.

However, in Philippians the word *parousia* does not describe Christ's coming, but rather Paul's presence. 'Therefore, my dear friends, as you have always obeyed — not only in my presence [*parousia*], but now much more in my absence,' Paul pleads, 'continue to work out your salvation with fear and trembling' (Phil. 2:12,13). Paul's presence sharpened spiritual awareness to a fine point; his influence was undimmed by absence. The apostolic presence promoted spiritual responsibility, according to Philippians 2:12. It is something like the teacher's presence in the class. Our Sunday School has lots of local children, some of whom are devoid of discipline. It is the teacher's presence that puts the lid on the pressure cooker of childish exuberance. In the

New Testament context, Paul's presence and the memory of his presence produced practical piety among the Macedonian believers.

Our word *parousia* pops up again in the first chapter of Philippians. There Paul posed the idea of a visit to Philippi, 'so that through my being with you [*parousia*] again your joy in Christ Jesus will overflow on account of me' (Phil. 1:26). Here again the Pauline presence is seen as being beneficial for believers. The apostle reached out to provincial Christians through various means. He extended a hand of fellowship in his God-given letters. In the process he penned almost half the New Testament. In other cases the apostle dispatched disciples to deal with needs in the church. One thinks of Timothy, Titus, Silas, Epaphroditus and a whole squad of apostolic errand boys. These godly men expressed Paul's parental concern and they brought back news about the churches. It was, however, the personal visit which best met the needs of the churches. The apostolic presence permeated the baby churches with discipline and delight.

Every pastor can understand this. When death rips away a relative, the caring pastor is immediately there. At the other extreme, when a baby is born into the family, a pastor finds great joy in leading the thanksgiving. When illness fells a church member, one drops everything and rushes to the bedside. This pastoral presence lends credibility to the pulpit ministry.

If the apostolic presence far outstripped our pastoral presence, how much more significant is the presence of the Lord! The word *parousia* is employed theologically to speak of the second advent. Then the Lord will be present in an unimaginable way. His presence portends a glory we cannot grasp. When he is present we shall sing the song: 'Worthy is the Lamb!'

Coming events

Each week advertising floods into our homes through the

Powerful presence

pages of the press, the medium of magazines and the television tube. The media have mastered the art of anticipation. Little trailers trip across the television screen leaving us longing for more. Whole pages publish the tantalizing, stylized message in our morning papers. (Even the so-called quality press is employed to produce full-page pressure.) By the time the product or service appears, the most resistant reader and viewer will risk a sampling. It is the anticipation which has whetted one's taste.

Our word *parousia* exudes expectation, too. Christ employed it when he answered the disciples' query: 'What will be the sign of your coming and of the end of the age?' (Matt. 24:3.) Paul predicted *parousia* when he wrote about those 'who are left till the coming [*parousia*] of the Lord' (1 Thess. 4:15). James spoke of it when he urged Christians to 'be patient . . . until the Lord's coming' (James 5:7). And Peter, too, referred to it when he wrote in answer to the sceptic's sneer: 'Where is this "coming" he promised?' (2 Peter 3:4). The coming of Christ is the beacon of hope which lightens our path forward. Christians are not sustained by faith only, but also by hope. Thomas Adams, the Puritan preacher and writer, put it succinctly: 'He that . . . rose from the clods, we expect from the clouds.' Stephen Travis underlines the truth in his little book, *The Jesus Hope*.[1]

A second use of the word *parousia* refers to *people*. Paul often wrote in this vein to churches. 'God, who comforts the downcast, comforted us by the coming of Titus' (2 Cor. 7:6). Paul also combated the misapprehension that 'his letters are weighty and forceful, but in person [*parousia*] he is unimpressive' (2 Cor. 10:10). Paul constantly underlined the salutary effect of apostolic and pastoral visitation. In ancient Greek literature our word *parousia* sometimes spoke of an imperial visit. Today we see this when the Queen or Prince of Wales visits a place. Usually there is a royal 'walkabout', and even the television cameras throb with the vitality of royal presence (*parousia*). Thus Paul knew his presence would have a positive effect on Christians. This explains Paul's restless and relentless 'get up and go'.

There is a dark side to our word. It speaks of the *parousia* of evil. 'The coming of the lawless one' (2 Thess. 2:9) anticipates the Antichrist. His coming will pre-date the *parousia* of the Lord. When I was a lad there was much teaching about the Antichrist. In fact, I shall not forget the Sunday evening when a powerful 'prophecy' preacher ascended the pulpit of our church. To a packed audience of several hundred, the speaker spoke of things to come. He flourished a blackboard and began to add up figures relating to the *Führer's* life. At the end Hitler was unveiled as the Antichrist. Subsequent history has erased that calculation, but not the fact of a coming Antichrist. His coming will unleash destruction unparalleled even by Hitler's butchers.

It is not the coming of Antichrist that animates me. Neither is it the appearance of a powerful person that pushes me onward in Christian service. It is the imminent appearance of the Lord that lights the way into the future. His *parousia* is my passion.

1. Inter-Varsity Press, 1974.

14.
Bent world

'Children of God without fault in a **crooked** *and* **depraved** *generation'* (Phil. 2:15)

In 1981 Ron Elsdon brought out his provocative book, *Bent World*[1]. As a geologist and lecturer at Dublin's University College, Elsdon has a broad knowledge of the ecological issues. He paints a horrific picture of environmental decline and he documents every assertion. As a convinced Christian, Elsdon is convinced that Satan's stirring has muddied the world's waters. The apostle Paul agreed with Elsdon (or vice versa). Our world is in a mess and sin is the source. When A. S. Way translated our verse from Philippians, he spoke of a world which is 'morally warped and spiritually perverted'.

Obviously there are two similar words involved. The word translated 'crooked' is *skolios*, and it speaks of something or someone who is 'crooked'. As in English this word has a literal meaning, like the bent nail I try to hammer into a board. Our word also has a figurative meaning: one speaks of a criminal as being 'bent' or 'crooked'. When I was a lad, one spoke of 'crooks' who were so 'crooked' that if they died they would be screwed into their grave.

The second word is translated in the NIV with 'depraved'. It is the Greek verb *diestrammenès*. It comes from the original verb *diastrapho*, to 'turn, turn around, convert'. In the Philippian context the word means to be 'turned to evil'.

Now we turn to the one verse in Philippians which contains both words. The first word, 'crooked', speaks of a situation in which people and things are bent out of shape. Like a horribly disfigured victim of burns, the face is twisted out of shape and people turn away from it. Even a smile or a kiss is repulsive. It reminds us of the old nursery rhyme:

> There was a crooked man, and he walked a crooked mile,
> He found a crooked sixpence against a crooked stile:
> He bought a crooked cat, which caught a crooked mouse,
> And they all lived together in a little crooked house.

The second term is equally unsavoury, for it speaks of 'depravity' or even 'perversion'. It is similar to the Scottish phrase 'thrawn', meaning to have a twist in it. Society is plagued with perversion. This is seen in ethical, moral, political, financial and even religious matters. In Greek the word was used to describe a piece of pottery which had been twisted out of shape. It was hardly a recommendation of the potter's prowess. He appeared to be clumsy.

One sees this same perverted depravity in our day. Recently I had a public correspondence with a prince of porn who operates a chain of sex shops. He argued that his sleezy shops fulfilled a socially necessary function, and I replied that they were about as helpful as an abscess is to a tooth. The whole exchange of letters showed me how twisted man's mind can be. But the same sort of sickness nauseated the apostle Paul in the first century. His, too, was a 'crooked and depraved' world.

Creation's twisted wreckage

There are many semi-humorous laws which have a germ of truth. Parkinson's Law says that work expands to fill the time available. The Peter Principle asserts that people usually rise to their level of incompetence. They progress through the ranks until they reach a level where they are totally incompetent. This slows down business to a snail's sprint. There is also a third law. It is Murphy's Law. Simply stated it is this: if anything can go wrong, it will. Even a well-kept car will ultimately break out in rust spots like metallic measles. Leave a garden alone, and it reverts to jungle in a matter of weeks. Give your teeth normal, quick care, and they soon succumb to decay. This law of degeneration was not devised by Murphy (whoever he was). It is the product of man's sin which spoils everything.

Let us look at our words in the wider New Testament context. The word 'crooked' is used both literally and figuratively. In Luke 3:5 we have a quotation from Isaiah 40:3: 'The crooked roads shall become straight.' Although this is Messianic prophecy, the idea is still literal.

A more figurative use is found in Acts 2:40, where the apostle Peter describes his contemporaries as 'this corrupt [crooked] generation'. Here there is a reflection of the Greek Old Testament version of Proverbs 21:8 and 28:18. A further application of the word is found in Peter's writings. Peter instructs slaves to co-operate with 'harsh' (crooked) masters (1 Peter 2:18). One of the very senior citizens (ninety-nine years young) in our church had a terrible stomach pain. When they admitted her to hospital a strangulated hernia was diagnosed. That twist in the intestine caused plenty of pain and an ominous threat. So serious was it that the surgeon operated − successfully. Well, the apostle here warns of the twists in man's make-up which pose a peril to his spiritual life. These can only be cut out by the Lord.

The second terrible twin word is translated 'depraved' or 'perverted'. In the Lord's language it had a moral implication. 'O unbelieving and *perverse* generation, the Lord lamented, 'how long shall I stay with you?' (Matt. 17:17.)

It is also capable of adaptation to doctrinal matters. When the apostle Paul bade farewell to the elders of Ephesus, he warned them of this: 'Even from your own number men will arise and distort [pervert] the truth in order to draw away disciples after them' (Acts 20:30).

The third application is even more spirit-chilling. When Barnabas and Saul set out across Cyprus they encountered the sorcerer Elymas at Paphos. Under Holy Spirit influence the apostle challenged him, because he 'tried to turn the proconsul from the faith' (Acts 13:8). He was also guilty of 'perverting the right ways of the Lord' (Acts 13:10).

There are many examples of perversion in our day.

Increasingly people try to widen the scope of the normal to include all sorts of perverted behaviour. However, the Bible is crystal clear in its ethical limits. An example is the creeping credibility given to homosexuality. In 1980 a Methodist study group came to the conclusion that homosexuality was a valid expression of human sexuality. They took the spiritual liberty from their view that 'Our Bibles cannot be directly equated with the word of God.'[2] Two years later the study group was still urging the Methodist Conference to approve the position 'that homosexuality is part of God's process of creative design'. In other words, that God is as pleased with homosexuals as he is with heterosexuals.[3] This grotesque giration to make sodomy saintly is nauseating. Furthermore it flies in the face of biblical revelation. Finally, it shows just how twisted man's mental processes are.

Like the first-century Christians in Philippi, we must shine like stars in the midst of a 'crooked and depraved generation'.

1. Inter-Varsity Press.
2. *The Times*, 1 July 1980.
3. *The Times*, 10 June 1982.

15.
Keep in touch

> *'To* send *Timothy to you soon'* (Phil. 2:19)
> *'I hope, therefore, to* send *him'* (Phil. 2:23)
> *'To* send *back to you Epaphroditus'* (Phil. 2:23)
> *'I am all the more eager to* send *him'* (Phil. 2:28)

Sending messages is big business. British Telecom in England has a growing and sophisticated network of radio, telephone and television links which keep us informed. Recently I met a tele-communications engineer who explained how thousands of telephone conversations are transmitted every minute, with very few crossed lines. To a scientific simpleton like me this seemed simply phenomenal. If one adds to the super-fast electronic communication the efficient postal system, there is a further multiplication of messages. Letters and packages speed to and fro every day and, amazingly, the vast majority reach the right address.

In the second chapter of Philippians Paul spotlights communication. His method is 'sending' special messengers with significant messages. Our focus falls on the simple word 'to send', or *pempo* as it is in Greek. So common is this term that it turns up seventy-nine times in the New Testament, and four of those references are in Philippians chapter 2.

First of all, Paul proposes to propel *Timothy*. 'I hope in the Lord Jesus to send Timothy to you soon', writes Paul, 'that I also may be cheered when I receive news about you' (Phil. 2:19). Just below this first reference, the apostle adds, 'I hope, therefore, to send him as soon as I see how things go with me' (Phil. 2:23). Obviously this tells us something about Paul's concern, but it conveys even more about Timothy. He is a ready messenger. Although communication was slower by personal emissary, it was no less satisfying than modern media. In fact, Paul here commends Timothy as an able ambassador. He is ready to go anywhere, to help anyone and to pay any price. Missionary history abounds with Timothy's spiritual soul brothers and sisters. One recent example must be C. T. Studd (1862–1931). The England cricketer sailed for China in 1885, only to be invalided home in 1894. Undaunted he served in India 1900–1906, before retiring through illness. This was only the prelude to his main work in Africa 1912–31. Like Timothy, Studd was God's messenger boy.

Paul paints yet another picture of this communication principle. This time the person is *Epaphroditus*. Paul finds it 'necessary to send back to you Epaphroditus', whom he lavishly describes as 'my brother, fellow-worker and fellow-soldier' (Phil. 2:25). After briefly writing about this Philippian brother, Paul says he is 'all the more eager to send him' (Phil. 2:28). Although Epaphroditus has fallen ill in Rome, Paul heaps praise on him. He is a 'brother' (Phil. 2:25), who shares the same spiritual parentage with Paul. As a 'fellow-worker' (Phil. 2:25) he is a valued 'mate' of the master missionary. Then he is further defined as a 'fellow-soldier' (Phil. 2:25), who has taken up arms against the onslaughts of Satan and his henchmen. In Philippians 2: 26–27 Epaphroditus is also a 'fellow-sufferer', because he had been struck down with illness while visiting Paul's prison cell. No wonder Paul recommends a hero's welcome for this battling believer! (Phil. 2:29,30.) My mind flashed to the missionary heroes I have seen. None is more fresh in my mind than Dr Coleman and his wife. As heroes of the Iranian hostage crisis in the eighties, they exemplified the courage for which Epaphroditus is known.

One further reference to 'sending' is in Philippians 4:16. 'For even when I was in Thessalonica', Paul recalled, 'you sent me *aid* again and again when I was in need.' Here is the generosity of gratefulness, as the Christians contribute to the support of their spiritual father. It recalls dozens of individuals who gave sacrificially to keep our family on the mission-field. And then there were several churches who stuck with us through plenty and poverty. Christians are always sending men and money as an expression of love.

God's transmitters

Sending is a strong New Testament emphasis. From the first, Christ compelled committed ones to go with the gospel. Many years ago there was a young couple serving as pastor in a nearby town. Increasingly the conviction ripened that they should go to South America. The wife penned a song which has become a missionary evergreen. The refrain brings the concept of sending into bold relief:

> Lord, send me,
> Oh, send me forth, I pray!
> The need is great.
> Thy call I will obey.
> Thy love compels me,
> I must go.
> I'm longing, ready,
> Willing to go.

This commitment to communicate flavours our word in its biblical expression. First the Lord sends *people*. When the Lord summarized his commission to the disciples it was in terms of sending: 'As the Father has sent me', he compared, 'I am sending you' (John 20:21). Such sending is always purposeful. One is sent to discover truth (John 1:22). On the other hand, one is sent to bear a message (John 13:16). John so loved this word 'send' that he used it thirty-three times in his Gospel – almost half of all the New Testament occurrences. Christian truth is carried along by sent people. At the end of his life the great preacher F. B. Meyer said, 'I have only one ambition: to be God's errand boy.'

A *message* is also sent. While waiting for the axe to fall, John the Baptist 'sent his disciples to ask [Jesus] : "Are you the one who was to come?"' (Matt. 11:2.) In the prologue to the Apocalypse John is told by the glorious Lord: 'Write on a scroll what you see and send it to the seven churches' (Rev. 1:11). When a message is sent, it is usually necessary. Our daughter lives in America. When she returns from a holiday with us in England, we wait eagerly for the message.

Instead of the usual letter, we normally resort to the telephone. God's message is even more important, and it is sent out by a multitude of messenger boys and girls.

Christ is also the Sent One *par excellence*. 'My food', explained Jesus to his disciples, 'is to do the will of him who sent me and to finish his work' (John 4:34). 'He who does not honour the Son', concludes the Lord, 'does not honour the Father, who sent him' (John 5:23). Christ was consumed with the concept of being sent by God. This gave him both the scope and the shape of his earthly ministry. As David Livingstone put it, 'God had but one Son. And he was a missionary doctor.'

A final turn to our word is the sending of the *Holy Spirit*. The Counsellor, the Holy Spirit, is the one 'whom the Father will send in my name', according to Jesus (John 14:26). One chapter later the same idea surfaces: 'When the Counsellor comes, whom I will send to you from the Father . . . he will testify about me' (John 15:26). Theological and physical blood has been spilled over the sending of the Holy Spirit. Does God the Father send him alone, or is God the Son involved in this momentous mission? Well, the Scriptures give aid to both sides. But the fact remains: the Holy Spirit has been sent to turn the dry kindling of human nature into the blazing bonfire of spiritual life.

God is a sending God. He sends us into our world as witnesses, just as he sent Jesus into the world as Saviour and Lord. Both Jesus and we are motivated by the Spirit's power. It is no wonder that we sing the simple chorus:

> Thank you, God, for sending Jesus,
> Thank you, Jesus, that you came.
> Holy Spirit, won't you tell me
> More about his lovely name?

16.
Soldier on

*'Epaphroditus, my brother, fellow-worker and fellow-***soldier***'*
         (Phil. 2:25)

Paul was surrounded by soldiers. In the Roman Empire of the first century there were thousands of men under arms walking around with shields and spears. Everywhere you looked there were soldiers. So even when writing under the Spirit's stimulation Paul was thinking about soldiers.

It is a little like the forties. When I was in my first four years of school a war was raging in Europe and the Far East. Our mums and dads talked ceaselessly about it, and we all had soldiers in the family. My cousin was a pilot, and my pride and joy was his cast-off flying hat. When we doodled we drew aeroplanes, tanks, guns and all those devastating devices of destruction.

In the same way, Paul picked military metaphors to describe spiritual truth. Epaphroditus, the home-town lad from Philippi who visited Paul was named a fellow-soldier. The Greek word is *sustratiotes,* and its root *strat* is seen in such English terms as 'strategy', 'strategic' and 'stratagem'. In our Philippian verse a prefix (*su,* meaning 'with') is added to further define the Philippian fellow as a 'fellow-soldier'.

The word is only used twice in the New Testament. (In Philemon 2 Archippus is likewise given the title of 'fellow-soldier'.) Paul wedded this word to other terms of affection. Epaphroditus was Paul's brother, showing the relationship of Christians to one another in God's family. From another angle Paul portrays him as a 'fellow-worker', who works at the same job with the apostle. This classes Epaphroditus with such notables as Apollos, Aquila and Priscilla, Aristarchus, Mark, Onesimus, Philemon, Timothy and Titus. All of these were likewise dubbed as fellow-workers of Paul. Furthermore, Epaphroditus was the 'messenger' (literally, 'apostle') of the Philippian church.

In this little chapter, however, we wish to concentrate on Paul's military metaphors. He made frequent reference to the Roman soldiers in this very letter. Although he was a prisoner subjected to the shame of that punishment, the palace guard had come to realize that there was a deeper meaning. 'It has become clear throughout the whole palace guard', Paul reported, 'that I am in chains for Christ' (Phil. 1:13). His first witness was to those surly soldiers who were chained to him as guards. They were sent to restrain him, but he was sent to evangelize them.

According to Paul, Christians were a force of elite troops extending the empire of Jesus Christ. They were constantly in combat with a Christless world, and they were following an invincible General, the Lord Jesus Christ. They were 'contending as one man for the faith of the gospel' (Phil. 1:27).

As Paul drew this little letter to a close he returned to his military model again. 'All the saints send you greetings,' he signed off, 'especially those who belong to Caesar's household' (Phil. 4:22). The witness which surfaced in the first chapter was fruitful. Many had been turned around, and even Caesar's court contained Christians. Perhaps this explains Nero's mania. You recall that Nero was so pressured by Christian advance that he set the city alight. We do not know whether or not he really fiddled, but we do know that he blamed Christians for the disaster. Then he unleashed a most bestial attack against Christians.

In many ways the first century was a century of conflict. The Roman rule was honeycombed with immorality and economic collapse. On the other hand, there was a virile Christian minority which moved relentlessly through the empire. By the dawn of the sixth century the Roman Empire had folded up and Christianity stood triumphant over the ruins of Rome.

Soldier on

Comrades in arms

Whenever old soldiers get together, they exchange war stories. Sometimes the stories are suspiciously like fishing tales, which have stretched in daring and adventure during the intervening years. Each year we hear remarkable yarns about the Dunkirk evacuation, when a flotilla of small boats plucked the English army from the French coast. 'Old soldiers never die,' declared General Douglas MacArthur after President Truman sacked him, 'they just fade away.' If past heroes fade from sight, many spiritual soldiers have found a place in the sacred Scriptures, and they never fade.

The word 'soldier' is used literally, usually referring to *Roman soldiers*. Although soldiers stripped the Saviour and threw dice for his clothes (Matt. 27:27,35), Roman soldiers often made a mark for good on the gospel record. The centurion who commanded the crucifixion squad saw the true nature of his victim. 'Surely he was the Son of God!' exclaimed the officer (Matt. 27:54). Earlier on in Christ's earthly life another Roman officer crossed his path. He pleaded with Jesus to heal a sick servant, and the people praised him as patron of the local synagogue. The Roman officer recognized Christ's superior authority when the Lord healed his servant from a distance (Luke 7:1-9). Of the exemplary imperial emissary Jesus said, 'I have not found such great faith even in Israel' (Luke 7:9). Cornelius was another commendable centurion. Doctor Luke penned this tribute to Cornelius in Acts: 'He and all his family were devout and God-fearing; he gave generously to those in need and prayed to God regularly' (Acts 10:2). And God heard his prayer by dispatching a rather reluctant Peter to preach the gospel to Cornelius and his clan. Yet another kind centurion was Julius. He was assigned to escort Paul on his prison journey to Rome. Of Julius the apostolic chronicler Luke wrote, 'Julius, in kindness to Paul, allowed him to go to his friends' (Acts 27:3). Most of the centurions in the New Testament were kind to Christians, and some of the soldiers also called on Christ for salvation.

In addition to the literal reference to soldiers there is

also the figurative picture of *spiritual soldiers*. In Paul's powerful plea for positive discipleship, he uses the picture of military training. 'Endure hardship with us like a good soldier of Christ Jesus', Paul challenged (2 Tim. 2:3). A soldier does not get involved with civilian pursuits. His top priority is obedience to the officer's command (2 Tim. 2:4). This single-mindedness was seen in Britain's recent Falklands conflict. Some soldiers left their brides virtually at the altar and sailed south to the conflict. Others left their wives to cope with the birth of a baby. As the troops returned home there were emotional scenes of burly dads cradling and cuddling babies born in their absence. Several reporters asked the returning soldiers this question: 'Would you go again if you were needed?' Invariably the men looked straight into the television camera and said, 'Of course I'd go back. It's my job.' They put their duty above their delight.

In the past hundred years there has been a corps of Christian soldiers marching forth to meet the needs of an urban industrial society. Under General William Booth the Salvation Army first set out with its band and Bible in 1878. Shortly afterwards Wilson Carlile mustered the Church Army in 1882 as an evangelistic army of the Church of England. In our day Operation Mobilization has emerged as a worldwide witness with the commitment of Christian commandos. It was the hymn-writer Sabine Baring-Gould (1834–1924) who put the principle into poetry when he wrote,

> Onward Christian soldiers,
> Marching as to war,
> Looking unto Jesus,
> Who is gone before:
> Christ, the royal Master,
> Leads against the foe;
> Forward into battle,
> See, his banners go.

17.
Watch out

> 'Watch out *for those dogs . . . men who do evil . . . mutilators of the flesh'* (Phil. 3:2)

Some things are worth watching out for. My first car was a 1955 Chevrolet. From it I learned to watch out for certain signs. One snowy winter night we were driving home through Chicago, when a yellow light appeared on the dashboard. Thinking it to be defective, I drove on. As we were slipping through the south side of the city, a horrible rumble erupted. It soon settled down into a knock and the car just stopped. The oil pressure had fallen below the acceptable norm and the engine — all six cylinders — just seized up. I learned to look out for warning signs.

That's the meaning Paul puts into a simple Greek verb *blepo*. Generally it means 'I see'. In this case, however, it means to 'look out' or 'beware'. Although the word occurs some 133 times in the New Testament and many times it sounds a warning, this meaning seems foreign to classical Greek.

Although the New International Version uses the word only once: 'Watch out for those dogs,' the other versions reflect the repetition in the Greek. For instance, the Authorized Version has: '*Beware* of dogs, *beware* of evil workers, *beware* of the concision.' And the Revised Standard Version says similarly, '*Look out* for the dogs, *look out* for the evil-workers, *look out* for those who mutilate the flesh.' The threefold repetition is true to the Greek.

First of all, the Philippians are to watch out for *dogs*. This is not an injunction for postmen to avoid pets, although that is good advice. Rather this refers to the vicious, disease-carrying scavengers which were so common in ancient times.

The Mosaic law called male prostitutes 'dogs' (Deut. 23:18 NIV compared with RSV). The psalmist called wicked men 'snarling dogs' (Ps. 59:6). Unconverted people who are excluded from the kingdom of God are likewise called dogs (Rev. 22:15). Jesus used a milder, diminutive word ('puppies' and 'pets') when he spoke with the Gentile Canaanite woman (Matt. 15:26,27). Dogs in a spiritual sense are those who 'worry the sheep'. Each spring dog-owners in Wales, Scotland and certain parts of England are warned to keep their dogs on a lead, lest they 'worry the sheep'. Spiritually speaking, Paul warns the Philippians to avoid 'dogs' who worry the Shepherd's sheep.

The second enemy mentioned is the *evil worker*. Already in Philippians 1:15,16 Paul warned of those who 'preach Christ out of envy and rivalry'. To the Corinthians he wrote warning against 'false apostles, deceitful workmen, masquerading as apostles of Christ' (2 Cor. 11:13). Some set out purposely to pervert the gospel and poison the Christians. It is much like the terrorist movement which has swept Europe in the past decade. The IRA and Protestant extremists have sabotaged society in the Emerald Isle. In Germany the Baader-Meinhof gang have murdered their way into the history books. To the south the Red Brigade have incited Italians to a siege mentality. These and many similar movements are 'evil workers', whose job is to destroy.

The third enemy is the *mutilator of the flesh*. Here Paul refers to the Jewish requirement of circumcision, which has been perverted into a saving act by the legalists. The argument which led to convening the Council of Jerusalem (Acts 15) was none other than this: must Gentiles be circumcised before they can be sanctified through Christ? At Jerusalem the consensus was contrary to legalism. Mutilation is not God's method of salvation. This is true whether it is the brainwashing of modern cults, or the addiction to marijuana among Rastafarians. God's way is spiritual healing, not physical abuse.

So Paul nails up a warning sign. 'Beware', he writes to the Philippians. It is good advice in the twentieth century, too. Let us beware of any spiritual scavengers who prowl around the churches nipping at the heels of God's people.

Sight-seeing

Let's broaden out the meaning of *blepo*. It refers generally to physical sight.

First of all, our word *blepo* means to see *people or things*. Jesus told John's disciples: 'Report what you hear and *see*' (Matt. 11:4). On the Mount of Olives Jesus said to his disciples, 'Do you see all these great buildings?' (Mark 13:2.) Jerusalem is impressive now, but in Jesus' day it was magnificent. From the hillside it was a 'sight for sore eyes'. The Christian sees the world and discerns his Creator's hand. Some years ago we took a tour to Switzerland. On a crisp, clear, cloudless day we took the cable car up Sentis, that great peak in north-eastern Switzerland. The sight is unforgettable and impossible to convey in words.

A second twist to our term is *seeing in contrast to blindness*. One recalls that riveting testimony of the man born blind. 'The man went and washed, and came home seeing' (John 9:7). Later he testified to the hostile Pharisees: 'One thing I do know: I was blind but now I see' (John 9:25). The statement is simple but the sight is startling. Recently we ministered to a woman whose husband died in his early thirties. Subsequently his corneas were grafted into the eyes of a young person, and now the recipient receives light through the eyes of a dead donor. That medical miracle is only a poor copy of Christ's miracle at the pool of Siloam.

A third application of our word is the one we saw in Philippians. '*Look out*' or '*beware*' is a distinctively biblical meaning of *blepo*. 'Watch out that no one deceives you,' Jesus told his disciples (Matt. 24:4). In another vein Paul prodded Archippus: '*See to it* [watch out] that you complete the work you have received in the Lord' (Col. 4:17). Christians are enjoined to watch out for many spiritual enemies. They are like the driver who takes the rigorous British driving test. At every stage of starting, turning, stopping and parking, the driver must watch all sides. This is the vigilance encumbent upon every Christian.

One final application of the word is *to see spiritual truth*. In linking faith and work, James urged his readers to 'see that his [Abraham's] faith was made complete by what he did' (James 2:22). Jesus was constantly deploring the fact that many had eyes but could not see spiritual truth (Matt. 13:13; Mark 8:18). A constant source of concern to the Christian is an unconverted person who simply cannot 'see' the gospel. Each week several sit in our services. They seem to enjoy the singing, experience the fellowship and they even endure the preaching. However, when pressed concerning the gospel, they simply cannot see it. Sadly some never see it.

So the admonition is apt. Open your eyes and see all God has in store for you. A new chorus recently caught on in our church, and it summarizes this little study:

> Open our eyes, Lord, we want to see Jesus,
> To reach out and touch him, and tell him we love him,
> Open our ears, Lord and help us to listen.
> Open our eyes, Lord, we want to see Jesus.

18.
Gains and losses

'Whatever was to my **profit** *I now consider* **loss***'* (Phil. 3:7)

'Profit and loss' is an electric phrase. Trot it out in a gathering of businessmen, and you are 'well away'. Everyone is interested in the profitability of business. For the top men it means bonuses, and for the shop-floor it should spell wage increases.

The Bible gives this idea a spiritual twist. People who produce profits for the money market often show a serious spiritual debit. 'He's no fool who gives up what he can't keep', mused the martyr Jim Elliot, 'to gain what he can't lose.' In other words, sacrificing the luxuries of life makes good sense if you are gaining life in the process. So seriously did Jim Elliot take this that he resigned the rat-race in North America for a missionary ministry in South America. It cost him his life, but he gained eternal rewards. So he could speak with some authority.

There are two Greek words in focus here. The word for gain is *kerdos,* and the verb form is *kerdaino.* It is in the plural form, so the emphasis falls on the individual things which were gain. Obviously, the second Greek word must be *zemia* for 'loss'. In contrast to the plural form of 'gains', 'loss' is just one single sacrifice. The emphasis falls on losing the whole thing at one time.

In sorting out the words separately, we shall first look at *kerdos*, 'gain'. Paul writes of all those things which he considered to be gain (Phil. 3:7). Here is the picture of a miser, letting gold coins flow through his fingers, feeling and fondling each one of them. Each hard-won gain is added to the growing heap. Paul was shocked to see that all of these gains were not worth a snap in terms of salvation.

Then he turns the word upside down and shows the 'surpassing greatness [of gain] of knowing Christ Jesus' (Phil. 3:8). When he piles up the privileges of Pharisaical Judaism on one side of the scales, he amasses the value of knowing Christ on the other side. The result is astounding: Christ outweighs all the benefits of being a Benjamite Jew.

Earlier on Paul had used the same word. For him 'to live is Christ and to die is gain' (*kerdos*) (Phil. 1:21). So Paul sorted out his priorities in terms of gain. Paul preferred what would gain the most for the longest period of time, indeed for eternity. And the embodiment of gain is God's Son, the Lord Jesus Christ.

From the encouraging concept of gain, we now turn to our second word *zemia* ('loss'). His previous position of power and prominence in Judaism turned out to be a 'loss' in comparison with Christ (Phil. 3:7). When stacked up against the Saviour, all else must be relegated to the rubbish bin as loss (Phil. 3:8). No self-made system of salvation can set us up for God's approval. All our best efforts are summarized in the withering word 'loss'. It is as though one would run around with a rubber stamp thumping every human effort with a big, red mark as 'loss'.

This strange upside-down look at human achievement is not too foreign to us. Recently I met a retired managing director of one of Britain's biggest firms. In his mid-fifties the man was broken in health and glad to be alive and actively retired. He had scaled the heights of the corporate mountain, only to find out that the sacrifice wasn't worth it. Gain had turned out to be loss. Two days later a missions secretary visited us. He had spent his life reaching and teaching gospel truth to Africans. Was it worth it all? A sense of accomplishment marked my missionary friend, despite his obviously modest life-style. Gain is giving one's life to God. Loss is keeping it for yourself.

Gains and losses

God's balance sheet

The rabbis tended to teach by contrasts, and our two words were an example. Comparing gain and loss can be instructive indeed. For instance, marriage means the loss of the single life, but the gain of married bliss is well worth it. Many people give up little luxuries to save for the purchase of a home. The loss of little things is more than offset by acquiring the home of one's dreams. The same is true of young people who give up earning money to prolong their education, which will bring benefit later. The Lord picked up the point, and it is recorded in all three of the synoptic Gospels. 'What good will it be for a man if he gains the whole world, yet forfeits his soul?' (Matt. 16:26; Mark 8:36; Luke 9:25.) Losing the lesser value is rewarded by gaining the greater.

The apostles presented gain in spiritual terms. Sacrifice was justified in Paul's mind, 'so as to win those not having the law' (1 Cor. 9:21). Christian wives aim to 'win' [gain] their husbands by a consistent Christian witness (1 Peter 3:1).

Material gain is uniformly discounted in Scripture. James warned of the man-made plan to 'go to this or that city, spend a year there, carry on business and make [gain] money' (James 4:13). But James warned against planning on tomorrow, because God has our times in his hands. Recently a young couple in our church became redundant. When they began to realize what was happening, they saw the plan of God. He was weaning them away from the obsession of 'building their own castle'.

Just as gain has both a material and a spiritual application, so has loss. Paul warned his captors to shelter over the winter rather than sailing for Rome. By God's enlightenment, Paul perceived 'that our voyage is going to be disastrous and bring great loss to ship and cargo' (Acts 27:10). Afterwards we find an inspired 'I told you so'. 'Men, you should have taken my advice not to sail from Crete; then you would have spared yourselves this damage and loss' (Acts 27:21). For the seasoned seamen of the

Roman merchant navy, ignoring God's man meant the jettisoning of cargo and the cracking up of the ship.

The corrupt Corinthians were warned by Paul to avoid spiritual loss. Faithless Christian workers would lose their life's work, although their soul was safe. Especially aiming at divisive teachers, Paul wrote, 'He will suffer loss: he himself will be saved, but only as one escaping through the flames' (1 Cor. 3:15). When we first settled in Germany I served as lay pastor of a small church. One day the senior pastor informed me of serious sin in our small congregation. The result was the excommunication of an offending brother and sister. The old gentleman had run well in the Christian life, but he had fallen at the last hurdle and landed in the swamp of sexual sin. His testimony and his fellowship in the church were both lost, a dreadful price for his foolish sin.

The Bible speaks in 2 Corinthians 5:10 of the 'judgement seat of Christ'. There Christians will be evaluated for both the good and the bad they have done. When that balance sheet is drawn up the gains and losses will be eternally entered. The obvious occupation of every Christian must be building profits for eternity and avoiding losses.

19.
Divine dynamic

'The power of his resurrection' (Phil. 3:10)

Recently local television carried some remarkable, although not unique, film. It focused on a nearby power station which was coming to the end of its productive life. One by one the soaring smoke stacks were being demolished. On a prescribed signal, the explosive charge was set off, and the chimney came down in a slow-motion collapse with dust and debris scattered all around. Weeks of work in erecting the stack were reversed in less than a minute, leaving only a pile of rubble as a reminder. The powerful impression was made by a simple explosive.

The Greek word for 'power' in the above-mentioned verse is *dunamis,* a close kin to our English words 'dynamite', 'dynamic' or 'dynamo', to name just a few. Although the noun *dunamis* ('power') only occurs about two dozen times in the New Testament, the verb form *dunamai* ('to be able', 'can', 'to have power') shows up no fewer than 200 times. Without being too simplistic, God talks about power in action and not as a state of being. Power is at work, not at rest, in the New Testament.

Power in the New Testament refers to the ability to overcome resistance. So the resurrection of Christ revealed his power to overcome the resistance of death. When a person believes in Christ, he is connected to the power of Christ's resurrection (Phil. 3:10). According to the apostle Paul, this involves resurrection from the death of sin (Col. 3:1), and subsequent life is marked by the buoyancy of resurrection (Col. 3:2). Christ was resurrected by the power of the Holy Spirit (Rom. 8:11), and that same personal Power permeates the life of the believer. Just as the massive Rolls-

Royce engines propel Concorde down the runway and into the air, so the resurrection power of Christ propels the Christian. This lifts him out of the gravitation of sin and into the stratosphere of salvation. Then the same power surges on until the Christian experiences sanctification and glorification (Rom. 8:30). It is Christ's resurrection power that overcomes the resistance in our lives.

A second occurrence of the root word is seen in this verse: 'The Lord Jesus Christ, who, by the power that enables him to bring everything under his control, will transform our lowly bodies' (Phil. 3:21). The theme continues here. Christ overcomes the decay of death and produces a whole new body for us in the resurrection. Again, the resistance of physical decline is reversed in a dramatic way. In the Soviet Union children are taught that Lenin is present. His spirit permeates all and he can be addressed in a grotesque caricature of prayer. In reality, however, Lenin is lying in the glass-covered coffin at the Kremlin. Christ, on the other hand, has overcome death and soared into the glory. Now he infuses us with that same resurrection power.

One final appearance of our word is this: 'I can do everything through Christ who gives me strength' (literally, 'empowers me') (Phil. 4:13). He not only personifies the power of resurrection, but he now lives to give me all the power I shall ever need. Like the little boy who put a horseshoe in a boxing glove to pack a punch, the Lord pours power into the weakest vessel.

The resurrection power of Christ covers our past with the blanket of forgiveness. Because of his resurrection power we look forward to a whole new body. In the meantime we live by the same power. Now that is dynamite.

Balance of power

Since 1945 the balance of power has been held by nuclear powers. Both East and West have held each other in check mainly by wiggling their finger on the nuclear switch. There has emerged a grim new twist to the age-old concept of

Divine dynamic

political balance of power. Now the peace protesters are questioning the whole validity of this crazy race.

In God's book power is essentially spiritual, and he has it all. The works of *God* are referred to as 'powerful deeds' or 'miracles' (Matt. 11:20—24). A miracle by sheer definition is an unleashing of divine dynamism.

When God reaches out to save someone, this too reveals his power. The gospel is described as 'the power [*dunamis*] of God for salvation' (Rom. 1:16). When one is converted to Christ the power of God the Holy Spirit streams into his life enabling him to cope (2 Tim. 1:7) and to communicate Christ (Acts 1:8).

God's power is without perimeter. There is no limit to what God can do. One sees this in the surging sea swell and the roaring thunderstorm and the delicate daisy. But one sees it more clearly in the conversion of men and women. Recently I heard that an estimated seven million enter the Christian church in Africa each year. Now not all are soundly saved, but a vast number are. Every day more than 20,000 join a Christian church, and one new church is opened each day of the year. That is God's power.

A second show of power focuses on *man*. In his parable of the talents, Christ claimed that God gave gifts according to a person's 'ability', or 'power' (Matt. 25:15). Paul spoke of enduring hardships 'far beyond our ability [power] to endure' (2 Cor. 1:8). And later in the same epistle he praised the Macedonians for giving 'as much as they were able, and even beyond their ability' (power) (2 Cor. 8:3). In other words, human abilities are reflections of the same Greek word, *'dunamis'* or *'dunamai'*.

Man's power is derived. He receives it all from God. This is true of special professional skills. But it is also true of the power to pump blood, the very working of one's heart. Many times I have seen a person stop breathing and the heart go into arrest. A medical person thumps the chest and the heart restarts. Is it the thump that works? Never! It is God whose power sustains even the basic functions of life.

There is a third perspective on power in the New Testament. The apostle Paul often referred to *angelic hosts* as 'power and dominion' (Eph. 1:21) or 'powers' (Rom. 8:38). The apostle Peter took up the same idea and spoke of 'angels, authorities and powers' (1 Peter 3:22). Angels, good or bad, have superhuman power. It is greater than ours but far less than God's. They have been around a lot longer than we have but only a short time by God's standards. They are superior beings, but superior only to us. Their power is limited by their Creator.

There is something vaguely comforting about this word 'power'. The reason is simple, because God has all the power in his safe hands. Even Satan cannot bring him down. In fact, in both the Old and New Testaments one of the Lord's names is just that, the Almighty.

20.
Caught by Christ

'To **take hold** *of that for which Christ* **took hold** *of me'*
(Phil. 3:12)
'I do not consider myself yet to have **taken hold** *of it'*
(Phil. 3:13)

Who caught whom is a constant source of debate in most marriages. The husband is dead certain that his spouse snared him. And the wife is equally insistent that her husband chased her. One wife put it this way: 'I chased him until he caught me.' In a happy marriage, both partners are glad they were 'caught', and it does not matter much who caught whom.

Paul takes this idea and elevates it to the realm of spiritual reality. He speaks of Christ 'taking hold' of him, and then he turns to say that he is in the process of 'taking hold' of spiritual truth.

The word used by the apostle is as common as dust in the New Testament. It is the verb *lambano* 'to take, take away, take hold, receive, choose, apprehend,' etc. The variety of uses is seen by the fact that this one single verb crosses the pages of Scripture 256 times. It also shows up with some linguistic partners. For instance, *katalambano* (to take down) which occurs in Philippians, speaks of 'seizing, winning or attaining'. And another combination verb is *paralambano* (to take from alongside), and this one is translated 'to take along or take over'.

In our text from Philippians, the verb simply sprouts up everywhere, like mushrooms in compost. 'I have not already obtained' *(lambano)* (Phil. 3:12). Then Paul changes over to the stronger, combined word *katalambano*: 'I press on to take hold of that for which Christ Jesus took hold of me'

(Phil. 3:12). And he is not yet finished with the idea, for in the next verse he writes, 'Brothers, I do not consider myself yet to have taken hold of it' (Phil. 3:13).

There is here a preoccupation with spiritual achievement. Paul is not standing still, although he is chained to a Roman guard. He is still climbing God-ward. He knows he has not yet arrived. He knows he is not yet perfect. Neither has Christ finished his sanctifying work in Paul's life. He knows what he does not know. If ever the Bible breaks the back of perfectionism it is here. The old story about a teenage lad bears repeating. At seventeen the boy thought his dad was dim beyond enlightenment. By the time four years had rolled by, however, and the young man came of age at twenty-one, he was amazed to see how much his father had learned in those four years. Paul shows a high degree of spiritual maturity here, because he knows well what he doesn't know, and what he hasn't achieved.

Our word *lambano* in some form occurs in two other Philippians passages. When describing the humanity of the Lord, Paul states that Christ took *(lambano)* to himself the very form of a servant (Phil. 2:7). Surely this was a prerogative open only to divinity. Only God become man could voluntarily take human nature. We have been stuck with it from birth. As a man Christ entered into every temptation and trial of human life, but he never sinned.

A second appearance of our word is in the final paragraphs of Philippians. In giving a final injunction the prisoner Paul urges his spiritual offspring: 'Whatever you have learned or received [*paralambano*] or heard from me, or seen in me – put it into practice' (Phil. 4:9). We often say that someone 'takes it in', although most pastors fear that their sermons often go right over people's heads. Paul urges his friends to follow what they have 'taken in'. During one winter we studied New Testament Greek with a small group of church members. It was a delight to see them take in the rudiments of grammar, although this was a hard slog. When we finally turned to translate the Gospel of John they took in some of the remarkable spiritual truths implicit in the Scriptures. All of us rejoiced together.

Paul was concerned that he might take in what Christ was doing in his life. And it is this 'gripping' message that still masters men and women who are open to the Lord.

Get a grip

One of the women in our church is a detective. On an afternoon off she went to have her hair done, and when she emerged from the hairdresser's shop she spotted a man she had been hunting. He likewise spotted her and took off with the detective in hot pursuit. Although the public kept a distance, refusing to lend a hand, the detective finally brought the culprit down with a tackle. She apprehended him.

Although the picture is violent, the idea is appropriate. Our word has two parallel lines of usage. First it is taken *literally*. The violent aspect of this verb is seen in the arrest and trial of Jesus. Judas took a detachment of soldiers (John 18:3). Pilate took Jesus and had him beaten (John 19:1). His garment was taken as the prize in a game of dice (John 19:23). There is a violent side to this verb, but there is also a more placid side. Christ *took* bread at the Last Supper (Matt. 26:26).

And the verb also has a *figurative* meaning. Jesus commends those who *receive* his words and he chastises those who reject them (John 12:48). One thinks of the hymn:

> Oh, make me understand it,
> Help me to take it in
> What it meant to thee,
> The Holy One,
> To bear away my sin!
> (Katherine A. N. Kelly, 1869–1942.)

The compound verb *katalambano* has several interesting meanings. It means to *win*. Paul often spoke of life as a race: 'In a race all the runners run,' he stated the obvious, 'but only one gets the prize' (1 Cor. 9:24). Paul was out to win the spiritual race and achieve the prize God had for him. Each year there is a heated competition between athletes from various lands. I enjoy the races, where one person pounds away until he is clear of the pack and then runs on to victory. This was epitomized in the film *Chariots of Fire.*

A second meaning of the compound verb is to *seize violently*. When Christ came into the world as light, the darkness tried in vain to seize it violently (John 1:5). When Christ comes again he will surprise dwellers in darkness like a thief, and the word translated 'surprise' is 'to take violently' *(katalambano)* (1 Thess. 5:4). In other words, the coming of Christ will give many people a nasty shock. A fact of life in our violent city is mugging. In fact, the street where our church is located was called by the local paper, 'Bristol's Street of Terror'. But the greatest surprise of all is not human violence but the unexpected coming of Christ.

A final use of our word is to catch or detect. The Pharisees were always prowling around trying to detect Jesus in some fault (John 8:3).

No better summary of our word is found than that of the apostle Paul. Let's paraphrase it this way: 'Christ caught me, and I'm still trying to catch on to the reason why he caught me. When I get to glory, I'll finally get it.'

21.
Perfect people

'Not that I have already ... been made **perfect***'* (Phil. 3:12)
'All of us who are **mature***'* (Phil. 3:15)

'Divine nature is perfection,' according to the ancient Greek writer Xenophon (434—355 B.C.), 'and to be nearest to the divine nature is to be nearest to perfection.' Although he was a pre-Christian essayist and soldier, Xenophon caught the Christian concept of perfection, but he missed the New Testament teaching on sanctification — how God makes us perfect.

In the Bible 'perfection' often reflects the Greek word *teleios,* which was discussed in *Living Words in Ephesians*[1]. Because of its prominence in Philippians, however, we now return for another consideration of *teleios*. In the New Testament our word is variously translated as 'having attained the end or purpose, complete, perfect', or even 'mature, fully grown'. The root idea of *teleios* is 'purpose', and it is seen in such English derivatives as 'teleology', the belief that any process is shaped by purpose. Life is not just the product of mechanistic fatalism. Anyway, our word speaks of purpose being fulfilled, perfection.

In Paul's autobiography he loudly disclaims that he is perfect. What he says exactly is this: 'Not that I have ... already been made perfect' (Phil. 3:12). Here the secret is in the verb. It is in the perfect tense and refers to action completed in the past. In other words, as yet Paul has not experienced perfection. God has not yet finished with Paul; there is still a lot of 'perfecting' to do in Paul's life. Paul knows very well that someday he will be sinlessly perfect. When he is 'with the Lord' he will be totally liberated from the load of sin and the lure of sin. Then he will really be sinlessly perfect. As Christians we believe that the moment our life ends on earth, we are whisked away to heaven. Then our soul is instantly perfected, for we are snatched out of Satan's reach once for all.

Although Paul denied that he was already perfect, he did speak of himself as being 'mature', literally 'completed, perfect' *teleios* (Phil. 3:15). The apostle put it this way: 'All of us who are mature'. In verse 12 Paul spoke of absolute, sinless perfection. In verse 15 he speaks of relative perfection, relative to the state in which we find ourselves. Thus it is perfectly permissible to speak of perfection. Everyone has said, 'That's a perfect baby.' What we meant was that for a baby, the present bundle of joy is unusually pleasing in intelligence, appearance or personality. Obviously if the baby fails to grow into childhood and adulthood, it is no longer perfect but rather imperfect or even retarded. So Paul, like Christians of every age, was not yet perfect. He was not absolutely free from the imperfections of humanity. But in God's eyes he was perfect or mature, having grown in the Lord. Most Christians cannot claim perfection on either of these counts.

Nobody is perfect

When a couple cruise down the aisle to be married, they are under the impression that both are 'perfect'. She is a 'perfect' bride. (With one or two exceptions, I have noticed that most brides are beautiful in face, grace and lace.) On the other side of the preacher stands a young man resplendent in his best suit, or the best suit he can hire. He is strong, well shaven and serious. They look like the proverbially 'perfect' couple, a marriage made in heaven. Later both learn that perfection is only skin-deep. A wife in hair-curlers compares unfavourably with the wedding photograph. And the husband doesn't stand up too well when he is unshaven, unsociable and uncouth.

That is the story of the human race, because none of us is perfect. We are not perfect in the final or absolute use of

Perfect people

the word. That perfection is only applied to God. Perfection pertains to the gifts God gives (James 1:17). When we submit to God's plan for our lives, we discover that he alone is able to plot out a perfect plan (Rom. 12:1,2). The Christian lives in the awareness of God's love, and that too is perfect (1 John 4:18). And God is thus able to issue this injunction to his people: 'Be perfect, therefore, as your heavenly Father is perfect' (Matt. 5:48). This is absolute, sinless and peerless perfection.

As such, we never see it in this world. When people look for a church home, they prefer a perfect church, only to discover that it is peopled with imperfect people. Along comes a spell-binding speaker with a perfect presentation of spiritual truth, but hearers are horrified to see that it is only imperfectly applied in the speaker's life. Another illustration is the loving Christian who seems to display perfect love, which upon further investigation seems to spring from imperfect motives. People are just not perfect, at least in the absolute sense of the word.

However, in the relative sense of the word, some are mature or complete. They are mature in the awareness of spiritual truth, and this presents them as being spiritually full-grown in relation to other Christians (Col. 1:28; Heb. 5:14—6:1). Other Christians have progressed in their attitudes from spiritual infancy to adulthood (1 Cor. 14:20). There is even the possibility of a whole church which has grown together into the unity of spiritual maturity (Eph. 4:13). (What a blessed prospect that is!) It is this mature Christian who eagerly looks forward to meeting the Lord with the assurance that he will be satisfied (Col. 4:12).

Relative perfection is seen in many human pursuits. A careful gardener can present a 'relatively' perfect rose, which will win competitions. Sportsmen likewise can achieve a high degree of perfection; one thinks of the ice-dance world champions Jane Torvill and Christopher Dean, who took the title in 1983. Christians strive, too, but for spiritual perfection. 'What is Christian perfection?' John Wesley introduced a subject of his special interest. Then he answered, 'Loving God with all your heart, mind, soul and strength.'

From the Puritan perspective Richard Baxter pointed out the importance of perfection. 'This life was not intended to be the place of our perfection,' Baxter concluded, 'but the preparation for it.'

1. p. 77.

22.
Sobbing saints

'I . . . now say again even with tears' (Phil. 3:18)

Tears mean trouble. The first time we took our toddler out she fell down and tears tumbled down her cheeks. In fact, tears seemed to mark every stage of childhood growth. When the infant was lovingly pushed out of the nest and into school, again tears marked the event. Teenagers seem to learn the art of turning tears on and off, almost at will. Even adults seem to use tears to soften up other people. Recently a famous movie producer won an Oscar for his film. He marked the event with a very soppy speech and a dash of tears to top it off. In this case it was tears of joy.

The Bible often speaks of tears, and the most common word is *klaio*, variously translated as 'weeping, crying', or even 'bewailing'. The Scriptures usually give credence to crying; it is usually a sincere emotion that wrings out the tear ducts, and the word occurs thirty-nine times in the New Testament.

In his letter to the Philippians Paul laments spiritual insensitivity. 'I have often told you before and now say again even *with tears,* many live as enemies of the cross' (Phil. 3:18). This marks a strange twist in the letter devoted to joy. Remember, this is the epistle which climaxes in that great Greek chorus: 'Rejoice in the Lord always. I will say it again: Rejoice' (Phil. 4:4).

So why does the apostle Paul speak of tears? He certainly is not weeping for himself. Although he was wearing chains in a Roman prison, he still wastes no tears on his situation. Neither is he weeping with fear. It is true that Nero has finally become completely insane. He would burn down Rome and blame Christians for the conflagration. He would use Christians as torches for his wild garden parties. Nero was well and truly mad, but Paul does not weep on this account.

Neither does Paul cry for the Christians at Philippi. He was grieved about the Corinthians and concerned for the Colossians and full of care for the Galatians, but the Philippian church was a model of Christian community life. No, Paul is not weeping over the foibles of fellow-Christians at Philippi. Neither is Paul sobbing because of the Jewish legalists. He is well aware that some boast of a better religious pedigree. They claim advantages because of the 'kosher' up-bringing (Phil. 3:2). They think themselves to be vastly superior to Paul and his band of Gentile believers. But Paul wastes no tears on these Jewish peacocks strutting around the embryonic church.

So who does cause Paul to weep? It is those people who are clueless regarding Christ. They disdain the cross of Christ, preferring to establish their righteousness by do-it-yourself methods (Phil. 3:18). Their whole life-style is locked up with lust. Whatever feels right is right. It is all a round of sexual experiment, self-indulgence and socializing. Finally, these Christless victims are orientated to this world. Their standards stem from the media. Their ethics are elastic, stretched to fit any situation. Their political preference is moulded by power and compromise. Paul puts it succinctly: 'Their god is their stomach' (Phil. 3:19).

Despite his own situation Paul is still outward-looking. As he views life in Rome he weeps over the non-Christians who are rushing to destruction (Phil. 3:19). Although he is moved to tears, the worldlings are not moved to repentance and faith, and for this Paul weeps. Why is it that we are so dry-eyed and spiritually sterile?

A time to weep

Weeping is linked in many minds with death. I remember my first funeral for an unconverted person. When the cortège rolled up to the crematorium mourners were already

Sobbing saints

mourning openly. As we commenced the short service the silent weeping turned to convulsive crying. By the beginning of my short address the dull, grey chapel echoed to the wail of grief. Never shall I forget that hopeless sobbing. The Scriptures catch something of this in their use of our word *klaio*, 'to weep vehemently'.

When the twelve-year-old daughter of Jairus died, the distraught father fetched Jesus to the scene. As he approached 'Jesus saw a commotion, with people crying and wailing' (Mark 5:38). The extremes of oriental grief were noteworthy even to Jesus, who had undoubtedly grown up with this display.

Another example of this sobbing is seen when 'Mary [Magdalene] stood outside the tomb [of Jesus] crying' (John 20:11). Literally, she was wracked with sobs as she stood there. Recently the local funeral director asked me to conduct a funeral for a young West Indian lad. After a violent clash with a policeman, the young lad had slit his throat. At the funeral and especially at the graveside the display of emotional grief was unforgettable.

Some say this overt expression of anguish helps to ease the burden of grief. Tennyson (1809–92) caught the tone of this grief when he wrote in *The Princess*:

> Home they brought her warrior dead.
> She nor swoon'd, nor utter'd cry:
> All her maidens watching said,
> 'She must weep or she will die.'

Weeping and grieving are linked inextricably.

But the Bible also associates weeping with *gratitude*. When the Lord was a guest in the home of the Pharisee Simon, most seem to have traded pleasantries and posed theological tongue-twisters. But behind Jesus stood a woman weeping. The men knew her as a sinner, but Jesus knew she had been saved. Her thanksgiving was poured out in the form of expensive perfume as 'she began to wet his feet with her tears' (Luke 7:38). The Pharisees pooh-poohed this expression of emotion, but Jesus saw it as the mark of her devotion and thanksgiving. One recalls many instances when a new baby has been born. When the parents look it over they discover the requisite number of fingers, toes, eyes and ears. As they gaze on that delightful but wrinkled little form tears trickle down their cheeks, tears of gratitude to God.

Then there are also tears of failure. The Bible records the denial of Jesus by Peter in prospect as Jesus prophesies it. Then it presents the dismal details as the event unfolds. Finally it flashes back to show the scene in grief. In the wake of the event Peter is heart-broken, and the Scripture records: 'He went outside and wept bitterly' (Matt. 26:75). These hot tears of grief marked the sorrow of Simon Peter at his own spiritual failure. Often I have seen someone return to the Lord after a period of backsliding. This is frequently marked by sincere tears of grief because of the time lost. As I write my mind focuses on a young man in our church, who recently returned to the Lord. He is tireless in his service for the Saviour, because he is making up for lost time.

A final occurrence of our word is spiritual *sadness*. As Jesus moved towards his triumphal entry into Jerusalem he paused, overlooking Jerusalem. Gazing at the beautiful city with the magnificent temple dominating the skyline, Jesus saw only the vast concentration of unbelief. 'As he approached Jerusalem and saw the city', Luke marks the details, 'he wept over it' (Luke 19:41). It was not the impending humiliation that drew tears from Jesus, but rather the stubborn refusal of the Jews to see their Messiah. They rejected their only Redeemer and the Romans harvested the city with Titus's sharp sickle.

Tears are part of existence on this earth. They have flowed from Eden right down through history to the present day. And they will continue to well up in our eyes as long as we live on this earth, but there is a better day coming for the Christian. In his Revelation road map to heaven the apostle John wrote, 'He will wipe every tear from their eyes. There will be no more death or mourning or crying or pain, for the old order of things has passed away' (Rev. 21:4).

23.
Political preference

'But our citizenship is in heaven' (Phil. 3:20)

'Religion and politics', according to most people, are the most divisive subjects in the world. In fact, one well-known popular women's club forbids its speakers to breathe a word about either their parochial or political preference. 'It might upset someone,' reason the leaders. And, of course, they're right. It does upset people.

In the verse mentioned above Paul takes politics by the tail and gives it a new twist. We are citizens of another commonwealth; our allegiance is to a heavenly order of things. The Greek word used for 'citizenship' is *politeuma*. It is easy to see the English equivalents of this word, because they all include some reference to 'politic'. Clustered around politics are such linguistic relatives as 'police, policies, politicians' and even 'polity'. All these words come from the Greek word for 'city', *polis*. And we see this in 'metro*polis*' and its twentieth-century big brother 'mega*polis*', literally 'great city'. The root word *'polis'* pops up no less than 159 times in the New Testament.

However, in our verse Paul is preoccupied with spiritual citizenship. 'Our citizenship is in heaven,' he teaches the Philippians (Phil. 3:20). Now they were a Roman colony with all the rights of Roman citizens. Their names were registered and they carried proof of this as a sort of ancient passport. They had a right to a proper trial if accused, and ultimately they could appeal to Caesar, as Paul did (Acts 25:11). They could move freely around the Roman Empire plying their trade. The Philippians knew a thing or two about citizenship in the Roman world, but Paul is now expanding that concept into a whole new sphere.

There is also a second occurrence of our idea in the Philippian letter. According to an earlier statement, Christians should 'conduct yourselves [literally, live as citizens] in a manner worthy of the gospel of Christ' (Phil. 1:27). Be good citizens of the commonwealth of heaven, Paul enjoins them. This shows the obligation of citizenship. Several years ago we lived in Karlsruhe, Germany. There were also stationed in that city about 11,000 Americans connected with the army. Soldiers had brought their families and there was a little American village on the slopes of the Black Forest. As we listened to the American Forces Network radio station, the soldiers and their wives were repeatedly urged to live exemplary lives. They were warned against the soldier's sins of 'wine, women and winnings'. The reason was always the same: 'Don't forget, you represent the United States.'

Paul writes to Christians who live in a foreign land. They are surrounded by the citizens of the world, who exert pressure to conform. Standards are set for the world not by a biblical basis, but rather by the overriding canon of expedience. Promotion does not depend on conformity to God's law. In contrast to this life-style, Christians stand out. They represent a dramatic contrast because they owe allegiance to a higher Ruler and they trace their citizenship to the kingdom of God.

My kind of town

Frank Sinatra summed up the feeling of many when he sang about Chicago, and the recurring refrain in that ode to the 'Windy City' is this one:

> My kind of town, Chicago is my kind of town.

In fact, most people wax lyrical about their favourite haunts. Another crooner, Tony Bennett, 'lost his heart in San Francisco', while Sigmund Romberg wrote of a similar experience in Heidelberg. From my home town, Detroit, comes a whole style of music known as the 'Motown' sound. The Beatles immortalized their Merseyside municipality.

This attachment to an earthly city is seen in the Scriptures, too. When the prodigal son spent all he had, he hired himself out to a citizen [*polites*] of that country' (Luke 15:15). Paul took pride in his home town Tarsus when he claimed: 'I am a . . . citizen of no ordinary city' (Acts 21:39). Let's be reminded that Tarsus was renowned as capital of provincial Cilicia, source of the goat's-hair cloth known as cilicium and home of a thriving university. It was indeed no ordinary city!

Civic pride is common all over the world. The beauty, cultural advantages and economic prominence of a city endear it to its residents, but there is more than that. From the Renaissance onwards people have enthused about cities. 'I have never felt salvation in nature,' mused Michelangelo, 'I love cities above all.' Even the German philosopher Georg Wilhelm Hegel (1770—1831) chorused the praise of cities: 'Only the modern city offers the mind the grounds on which it can achieve awareness of itself.' So from the apostle Paul right down to the present, there is a mystique about citizenship in a city.

But the Scriptures plumb deeper depths of meaning. They attach great value to citizenship of the heavenly city. When writing to residents of the great city of Ephesus, Paul pointed them heavenwards: 'You are no longer foreigners and aliens, but fellow-citizens [*polites*] with God's people and members of God's household' (Eph. 2:19). Formerly they had another allegiance which excluded them from 'citizenship in Israel' and disconnected them from 'the covenants of the promise' (Eph. 2:12). So becoming a believer attached one to the commonwealth of Christ and the kingdom of God.

In the Westminster Abbey of faith we find many pilgrims processing through history to eternity. None is more prominent than the human leader of that parade, Abraham. He, too, talked about citizenship. 'He was looking forward to a city [*polis*] with foundations, whose architect and builder is God' (Heb. 11:10). The roving example of justification by faith knew that the best was yet to come, when he settled down for eternity in the kingdom.

In 1831 Lady Powerscourt invited the early Brethren to a conference on prophecy on her Irish estate. These conferences focused much attention on Bible prophecy, a subject of sincere interest to the noble woman. F. B. Meyer quoted Lady Powerscourt on the subject of spiritual citizenship when he said, 'The Christian is not a man who, standing on earth, looks up to heaven; but who, being in heaven, looks down upon earth, and throughout his life he recognizes that he is a foreigner indeed.'

The famous bishop Augustine of Hippo (354–430) wrote about this citizenship in his *City of God*. When the barbaric Alaric sacked Rome in 410 Augustine lifted the eyes of Christians away from the 'eternal city', so recently razed, to the real eternal city of heaven, which is never under threat. That is the city of which we, too, are citizens.

24.
Winner's crown

> *'My brothers . . . whom I love and long for, my joy and crown'* (Phil. 4:1)

When an athlete outstrips all the competitors he has a gold medal hung around his neck. Some, like the legendary Olympic swimmer Mark Spitz, have several medals. If a boxer beats all his challengers, he gains a belt. The ornate belt with a valuable buckle proclaims the prowess of the puncher. In racing the triumphant driver or rider often receives a wreath. He hangs it around his neck or the horse's. It is the winner's wreath that marks the master.

When the apostle Paul penned his letters the Greeks were sports mad. The Olympic Games had been a tradition for more than 800 years, and they endured until the fourth century of the Christian era. Paul kept referring to sports and comparing Christian living with a race (1 Cor. 9:24).

The prize for winning in Greek games was a wreath of laurel, a *stephanos*. So popular was this prize that it was also passed out to military victors and participants in special events. Usually it was woven together from laurel, oak and ivy. Sometimes there were flowers added, such as violets or roses. The Greek word *stephanos* is reflected in our proper name 'Stephen'. The laurel wreath, *stephanos*, is often translated 'crown' in the New Testament, but its meaning is always the same: a mark of triumph and a reward for achievement.

Incidentally, there is another word rendered with 'crown'. This one is *diadema,* or 'diadem'. It is the mark of royalty and indicates one's position, rather than one's achievement *(stephanos).*

However, it is the laurel wreath of achievement that Paul

mentions in Philippians. Christians are his laurel wreath. When it comes to God's final summing up, Paul's only reward will be those whom he has influenced for Christ, those who were won through his life. These are his 'joy and crown' (Phil. 4:1).

In fact he lavishes descriptive honours on these Philippian saints. First he calls them 'my brothers' (Phil. 4:1). No less than seven times in the short span of the Philippian epistle Paul refers to Christian brothers. They understood Paul's plight (Phil. 1:12). When he was side-lined, they took up Paul's work (Phil. 1:14). Despite his imprisonment, they were privy to Paul's innermost feelings (Phil. 3:13). In accordance with his instruction they followed Paul's example (Phil. 3:17).

Now the relationship between brothers is not a matter of choice. We don't choose our family, and they don't choose us. Otherwise there would be a lot more orphans in the world than there are! By the same token, God brings us into his family by the new birth, and this relates us to a whole host of spiritual brothers who share our lives.

A second term tied to these spiritual soul brothers is the phrase 'loved ones'. In the New International Version it is translated in two ways: those 'whom I love and long for' and 'dear (literally "loved") friends' (Phil. 4:1). Paul longs for these beloved fellow-Christians. The word translated love is *agape,* God's super love.

In our day we have a special strong adhesive known as epoxy glue. It holds with an especially strong bond, and there have been some painful accidents with it, like the child who stuck his eyelid shut or the man who glued his finger to a teacup. God's love is a binding agent which unites Christians more strongly than mere human love *(phileo)* or superficial sexual love *(eros).*

Another name for Paul's crowning glory, his brothers, his loved ones is 'his joy' (Phil. 4:1). In a new popular series of commentaries Warren Wiersbe named his commentary on this epistle *Be Joyful.* Joy is a dominant theme of Philippians. The reason for Paul's joy is simple: it is the Philippian Christians themselves.

Recently I met a former student. He is a tall man and a

handsome chap. His spiritual life simply radiates from every pore. As soon as he spotted me he flung those long arms around me, right in front of the railway station. What a joy he is! That is the kind of joy Paul speaks of here. The crowning touch of any ministry is not a title, or a full church, or a rich treasury or even a stack of erudite books. The crown of our ministry is people transformed by God's grace, related through his family, throbbing with God's love and radiating his joy.

God's prize-giving

From the commencement of my academic career I have attended many graduation exercises or prize-givings. It was a hot August day near Chicago when I made my dignified way across the platform resplendent in my robe, only to hear our infant daughter call out, 'Daddy'. Another occasion was the Bible College prize-giving, when I learned I was responsible for giving a 'Greek Prize' to the best student. In fact, that college was obsessed with prizes for everything from academic survival (the student who showed the most improvement) to spiritual promise (the student who was 'most spiritual').

God's prize-giving relates to our ministry. His prize is first and foremost the *people* who have been won for him. 'For what is our hope, our joy, or the crown in which we will glory in the presence of our Lord Jesus Christ when he comes?,' and then Paul answers in one short sentence: 'Is it not you?' (1 Thess. 2:19). These are a crown which will last for ever (1 Cor. 9:25). Professor Merrill Tenney was my revered New Testament teacher. He opened masterfully the pages of Scripture to many generations of more or less gifted students. However, Professor Tenney often said to us, 'You are the proof of my ministry.' He sincerely believed that some would outstrip him in influence for the gospel, and some have indeed. They are the 'crown' of his ministry.

A second aspect of God's prize-giving is *ultimate reward*. As he put the final touches on his life's work, Paul spoke of his reward. It was seen in terms of a 'crown of righteousness' (2 Tim. 4:8). Peter promised that the Chief Shepherd would award every faithful servant 'the crown of glory that will never fade away' (1 Peter 5:4). Now this reward is not a gratuity; it is deserved. In 1982 Britain mounted a military operation to liberate the Falkland Islands from Argentina. Afterwards there were television pictures of heroes, or their widows and parents, receiving rewards from the Queen. When we serve Christ, no earthly queen would consider us for an award, but the heavenly King knows all about it. His laurel wreath will never wilt.

A third use of our word *stephanos* is obviously the *proper name*, Stephen. In Acts 6 and 7 we have the record of that remarkable man. Chosen to serve the saints, he served by the sacrifice of his life. His crown was not only a worthy name, but the mark of martyrdom. One could wish that every young man who bears the name of Stephen and every girl called Stephanie would bear the crown of God's approval. As I write, we have just sent off a lad for short-term service. He is 'Stephen' in name and reward.

Finally, the word *stephanos* takes an ominous twist. When the Lord was tried he received a wreath, *a crown of thorns*. The soldiers 'wove a crown of thorns and set it on his head' (Matt. 27:29). Ironic is it not, that the one who deserved the crown of glory should be scorned with a crown of thorns? While on tour in Israel we saw those Palestinian thorns. They were not short little prickly things, like the thorns on a rose bush. No, the Middle Eastern variety were an inch long at least and as hard and sharp as a spike. Those were the thorns jammed down on the brow that bore our sin.

It took the skill of a hymn-writer to catch the significance of Christ's crown of thorns. Thomas Kelly (1769–1854) wrote 765 hymns in all, and none is greater than the one which says,

> The head that once was crowned with thorns
> Is crowned with glory now;
> A royal diadem adorns
> The mighty Victor's brow.

25.
Plea for peace

'I **plead** *with Euodia and I* **plead** *with Syntyche'*
(Phil. 4:2)

Every motorist knows the panic of a breakdown. It was a chilly spring evening when my usually reliable car quit. Miles from nowhere and short of change for the phone, I felt desperation rise like nausea in my throat. Finally I found a service station willing to give breakdown service. The rather surly mechanic looked at my maimed motor and made clucking noises.

'Oooh!' he muttered, drawing in air ominously. 'There's nothing I can do tonight,' he said almost gleefully, 'it's the water pump that isn't pumping.' An expensive night in the hotel and a more expensive repair job later, I was on my way home. Although I am sure he took me for a ride, I was just glad to be going again.

It is this idea of emergency and urgency that permeates the Greek word we consider here. 'I plead,' Paul said, and the word translated 'plead' is *parakaleo*. This rather common verb gave its name to the Holy Spirit, the 'Paraclete'. Literally it means 'one who is called alongside' to help. Practically it appears in such contexts as 'exhorting, comforting, imploring' and 'pleading'. The verb shows up more than a hundred times in the New Testament, and we look at its appearances in various contexts.

When Paul turned the corner in Philippians and headed towards the conclusion of his letter, he mentioned one little cloud on the horizon of the Christian community. The problem was dissension between Euodias and Syntyche. 'I plead with Euodia and I plead with Syntyche,' Paul wrote, 'to agree with each other in the Lord (Phil. 4:2). Who were these ladies? The New Testament gives us no clue. What was the cause of their disagreement? Again the Scriptures are silent. But the necessity for restored unity is foremost in the apostolic assessment of the church.

The unity for which Paul pleads is a far cry from contemporary ecumenical efforts. Church union today is based on organizational compromise and doctrinal surrender. As Sir Fred Catherwood concluded, the ecumenical movement is a 'pooling of poverty'. The Pauline picture of unity was spiritual. It arose out of life 'in the Lord' and issued in 'contending for the cause of the gospel' (Phil. 4:3). The fulfilment of this unity focused on heaven, where God keeps the books (Phil. 4:3).

A second appearance of our word *parakaleo* popped up in Philippians chapter 2. 'If you have any *encouragement* from being united with Christ,' Paul introduced the subject of spiritual oneness (Phil. 2:1). Here the verb *parakaleo* means to encourage or comfort. How close this comes to the comforting ministry of the Holy Spirit! He is pre-eminently the 'one who is called alongside' to comfort and encourage us.

Christians are companions in comfort. Recently Josef Ton, the exiled Romanian Baptist pastor, preached in our church. His spiritual impact left an indelible mark on our hearts. One memorable remark was the statement that persecuted pastors derive inestimable aid from the prayers and correspondence of other Christians. Also, the commissars of cruelty are impressed by the support Christians confer upon their suffering sisters and brothers. The worldwide communion of Christians is a medium of Christian comfort and an embodiment of the Paraclete, the Holy Spirit.

Call for help

Living as we do in an island nation, we are well aware of sea disasters. When a Dutch coaster was caught by a storm it struggled in vain. Finally the 'Mayday' message was sent and the Penlee lifeboat was launched. But the crews of both coaster and rescue vessel were lost. The SOS was serious and the lifeboatmen were valiant, but the storm won and it cost the crews their lives.

Our word *parakaleo* pops up a hundred times in the New Testament, and it is always associated with urgent communications. First, it means to *implore or beg.* In his home town of Capernaum a centurion caught Christ. According to the New International Version, the centurion was 'asking for help' (Matt. 8:5). The Authorized Version captures the flavour of *parakaleo* when it says the centurion was 'beseeching' (imploring) the Lord.

In his intensely personal letter to Philemon the apostle Paul again employs our word. 'I appeal [*parakaleo*] to you for my son Onesimus', Paul wrote to his friend Philemon (Philem. 10). This persuasive version of our word is always positive. It is the doctor seeking to persuade a heart-attack victim to lose weight. The goal is good and the persuasion is born of concern.

A second aspect of our word is *exhortation.* When he wrote to the Thessalonians, Paul exhorted them to 'live lives worthy of God' (1 Thess. 2:12). Later on he instructed them to 'encourage one another and build each other up' (1 Thess. 5:11). The most urgent exhortation is in his Corinthian letter, where Paul says, 'We *implore* you on Christ's behalf: Be reconciled to God' (2 Cor. 5:20).

A final meaning of our word is *comfort.* 'Blessed are those who mourn,' Jesus taught on the mount, 'for they will be comforted' (Matt. 5:4). Elsewhere the saintly Simeon described Messiah's advent as 'the consolation of Israel' (Luke 2:25). True comfort is connected to Christ and contained in the Holy Spirit and fulfilled in God the Father. Comfort or consolation is primarily the prerogative of God.

Comfort is not pious platitudes but a Person. It is like when a small child cries out in the night. No parent will forget the feeling. You awaken in the blackness of night. Your tongue feels as though it is wearing a Shetland sweater. For a moment you think it is all a nightmare. When your feet finally reach the floor they almost freeze. At last you reach the child's bedside and the crying stops. Comfort is the presence of a parent. It is not soothing words but the sweet presence of a loving father or mother.

Thus our true *paraklete* is the Holy Spirit. A Christian collects comfort not from religious instruction or even good advice. Neither does a Christian derive consolation from pious platitudes. No, the Christian's comfort is the presence of his Lord.

26.
Joy way

> 'Rejoice *in the Lord always. I will say it again:* Rejoice!'
> (Phil. 4:4)

'When I think of God', wrote Franz Josef Haydn (1732–1809), 'my heart is so full of joy that the notes leap and dance as they leave my pen.' Then he added the reason for this delight: 'Since God has given me a cheerful heart, I serve him with a cheerful spirit.'

There is Christian joy in a nutshell. The source of our joy is the Lord and the expression is found in every event of life. In the previous chapter I mentioned the Romanian Josef Ton, who preached at our church. He told his secret for surviving severe persecution. Once the mercenaries of misery caught him out. While they were badgering the preacher, he was meditating on hymns and inadvertently he smiled. The cruel consequences can be imagined. His mind was maintained by the joy of the Lord.

Our word 'joy' is a translation of the Greek noun *chara* or the verb *chairo* (I rejoice). As can be imagined, the word is found frequently in secular and sacred literature. Simply, it means to be glad, but it is also employed as a greeting, 'welcome, good-day, hail', or even 'a festive dinner'.

'Joy' is the predominant point of Philippians. When he wrote his popular commentary on the epistle, Guy King called his slim volume, *The Joy Way*. Writing in the eighteenth century, Johann Albrecht Bengel (1687–1752) said joy is the 'sum total of this epistle'. The famous *Expositor's Greek Testament* agreed: 'Joy expresses the predominant mood of Philippians, a mood wonderfully characteristic of Paul's closing years.'

The word 'joy' or 'rejoice' shows up several times in

Philippians, but the most outstanding appearance is our verse: 'Rejoice in the Lord always. I will say it again: Rejoice!' (Phil. 4:4.) Here Paul departs from good advice and gives a positive exhortation. His aim is to catapult Christians out of their circumstances into Christian joy. In the words of the Puritan writer Walter Craddock, 'Take a saint, and put him into any condition, and he knows how to rejoice in the Lord.'

The remaining references to joy in Philippians cluster around three main themes. First, there are purely *spiritual joys*. Paul thanks God for the Christians as he 'prays with joy' (Phil. 1:4). No matter what motive moves people to preach the gospel, Paul rejoices that Christ is preached (Phil. 1:18). When Paul perceives the progress of his Philippian brothers and sisters in the faith, this, too, fills both them and him with joy (Phil. 1:25,26). Nothing increases joy like gospel partnership. This is a pure joy springing up like an artesian well.

A second segment of references speaks of *social joys*. When Christians cling together, this increases the apostle's joy (Phil. 2:2). Sympathetic identification between the Christians and their spiritual father likewise increases joy (Phil. 2:18). And the return of absent brothers to the warmth of Christian welcome also widens joy (Phil. 2:28,29). Joy is the safeguard of Christian community (Phil. 3:1) and the reward of Christian service (Phil. 4:1). In all the above cases, the source of joy is fellow-Christians. In our day we often find Christians to be cantankerous and critical, but Paul prided himself on the joy generated by Philippian brothers.

The final facet of joy is *service*. This is emphasized in the apostle's farewell to the Philippian Christians. Their renewed concern for him and generous gift to him has caused him to 'rejoice greatly' (Phil. 4:10). When Christians minister to one another this is genuinely encouraging.

Some years ago I was lecturing in Sweden during the autumn. Each day was darker and more dreary than the one before. One student told me they were praying for snow, and I almost laughed. Then one morning I saw what

Joy way

they meant. When the sun crept up over the horizon in late morning, the ground was covered with lovely fresh white snow. Immediately the whole landscape brightened up, and so did our spirits. The joy of the Lord brightens the blackest day and the most dismal saint.

I've got the joy

Years ago and half a world away when I was a lad we used to sing a little Sunday school song about joy:

> I've got the joy, joy, joy, joy
> Down in my heart to stay.

The words were trite and the tune terrible, but the truth is unassailable. Christians who have been conquered by Christ have a joy which most of the world can never comprehend.

The trouble is this: few let the joy show. I've watched charismatic Christians enthuse about the 'renewal' while their faces looked like a mud fence after ten days rain. On the other hand I have heard Reformed brethren extol the sovereign grace of our God and never crack a smile. When we were in Germany we used to participate in Lutheran liturgy which at one stage included the glorious exclamation, 'Hallelujah!' You should have seen the sullen, smileless faces of those 'rejoicing' worshippers.

Our word 'joy' strikes deep into the emotions of believers. It speaks most obviously of *gladness*. The same apostle admonished Roman Christians to 'rejoice with those who rejoice' (Rom. 12:15). The source of this delight is none other than the Holy Spirit, who pours out peace and joy (Rom. 14:17; Gal. 5:22,23). When the Gentiles heard the gospel, 'they were glad and honoured the word of the Lord' (Acts 13:48).

Now I wonder what has happened to the church of Jesus Christ since the first century. The joy of the Lord has been clouded over, and all that can be seen is big black clouds of gloom. When Christians congregate they should be rejoicing in the Lord. Instead they organize an organ recital, which swaps stories about the latest gall bladder or stomach surgery.

The second meaning of our word in the New Testament is a *greeting*. 'Greetings' (literally, 'rejoice'), 'you who are highly favoured', the angel announced to Mary, 'the Lord is with you' (Luke 1:28). Another twist to this greeting is the mockery of Jesus as a candidate for crucifixion. 'Hail', (literally 'rejoice') 'King of the Jews!' the Romans taunted him (Mark 15:18).

In many countries the greeting is an implicit commitment to God. *'Grüss Gott'*, the Bavarian chirps, and it means literally, 'God greet you'. South of the border the Spaniards wish you *'adios'* or 'go with God'. In France there is a similar greeting, *'adieu'*. The English often say: 'Cheerio' or just plain 'cheers'. Anyway, the meaning is the same, a wish for joy.

The final fixture is an unusual meaning for our word. In some cases it is translated as a *festive meal*. When he winds up history, the Lord will say to his servants: 'Well done, good and faithful servant! . . . Come and share your Master's *happiness*' (Matt. 25:21,23). Elsewhere it is called the 'marriage feast of the Lamb'. Heaven is portrayed as a gala event with the Lord as the centre-piece. He is the Host, and he is also the Light. No other person in paradise can hold a candle to Christ. It is his dominion, and his people will have a share in it. Recently our son became engaged and we went out for a festive meal. Slightly embarrassed, I explained it to a Christian doctor friend. 'Well done,' the senior brother encouraged me. 'Every family event should be celebrated in style. Make the most of the Lord's joy.'

And that is why Paul persuaded the Philippians to 'rejoice in the Lord always'. Then the inspiring Spirit gave the jailbird apostle another nudge and he wrote, 'I will say it again: Rejoice!' (Phil. 4:4.)

27.
Prayer power

'Prayer and petition with thanksgiving' (Phil. 4:6)

Recently a royal steward landed himself in the soup. After serving Queen Elizabeth for a few years, Paul Kidd moved to Manchester. His shocking revelations appeared in *Decision* magazine, and they revolved around a startling confession. Mr Kidd had actually led prayer meetings in Buckingham Palace, and he preached to visiting ministers of the Crown, too. Paul Kidd even set up a prayer cell aboard the royal yacht *Britannia*. It was all right to pray, but he broke royal protocol when he wrote his article. *The Times* was shocked by this revelation.

On the B.B.C. another shocking revelation emerged. A visiting American speaker, Mrs Evelyn Christianson, was interviewed about her ministry of encouraging prayer. (She wrote the book, *What Happens When Women Pray*?) The shocker was a story pried out of her by a rather sensation-seeking interviewer. Along with other Christian leaders, Mrs Christianson was approached by the White House, when President Reagan asked them to pray for him. 'Wasn't the President embarrassed by your prayers?' the nonplussed newsman asked.

So prayer is still making headlines. In the verse mentioned above there is a triplet of terms which describe our conversation with God. 'Prayer' is the general term for adoration and worship, the Greek word *proseuchomai*.[1] The word translated 'thanksgiving' is really *eucharisteo*, which gives us the English word 'eucharist'.[2] It is, however, the third word for prayer which we here slide under the microscope, the word 'petition' (Greek *deesis*). It is translated with such strong synonyms as 'entreaty, request, supplication'.

115

In fact, our word crops up three times in Philippians. In the verse under consideration, we are urged to be anxious about nothing, 'but in everything, by prayer and *petition*, with thanksgiving, present your requests to God' (Phil. 4:6). Prayer is propelled out of the plane of pointless repetition on to the level of daring declaration. Every need of our lives is elevated to a request to God. We need never worry about wasting God's time, because he instructs us to come with these concerns. Recently we were contemplating a change in ministry. Nothing seemed to come clear. When we dedicated a day to prayer and fasting the future became immediately clear, like a landscape when the morning mist is burnt off by the sunshine. God's grace dispelled the gloom and gave us a clearer vision. Prayer was the key which prepared us to see God's way.

Our word *deesis* also appears in the early verses of Philippians. 'In all my *prayers* [or petitions] for all of you', Paul wrote, 'I always *pray* with joy' (Phil. 1:4). When Paul presented the Philippians to the throne of grace, he was joyful about all of them. During my final year at Kensington in Bristol I taught at Trinity College, the Anglican theological establishment. Needless to say, this was a mind-stretching experience, but it was also a joyful one. The students were true fellow-foragers in the truth of God. Whenever I think of them, I rejoice and thank our common Lord.

Paul not only prayed, he asked for prayer. 'I know that through your *prayers* and the help given by the Spirit of Jesus Christ', he concluded, 'what has happened to me will turn out for my deliverance' (Phil. 1:19). Paul did not believe that prayer was pointless or powerless. He knew that God worked as a direct result of prayer, and the apostle ascertained this by experience.

A humorous example of this appeared in the national newspapers. At a bankers' banquet in Newquay, Cornwall, the Bishop of Truro, Peter Mumford, was engaged to give thanks. When he stood to pray the assembled financial feeders were amazed and amused, for the bishop prayed, 'O Lord, grant that we may not be like porridge — stiff, stodgy and hard to stir — but like cornflakes — crisp, fresh and ready to serve.' Not that I would dare do it, but the sentiment is spot on. Prayer presupposes that God can and will change us and our circumstances. That is why we petition the throne of grace.

Prayer or paralysis

The thrust of Philippians is Paul's answer to anxiety. His medicine for mangled spirits is prayer. At a recent meeting of medical brains a Harvard University professor startled the sleepy scholars. Prayer is a powerful antidote to stress, according to Professor Herbert Benson. It heads off heart attacks, brings down blood pressure, stops hammering headaches and even suppresses the pain of cancer. Professor Benson brought out these 'new' discoveries at a conference on 'New Directions in Health' held in London during April 1982.

Now preacher Paul and doctor Luke knew this two thousand years ago. 'You help us by your *prayers*,' Paul told the Corinthians (2 Cor. 1:11). Prayer worked and Paul knew it. So did Samuel Chadwick. 'Satan is not afraid of prayerless study, prayerless work or prayerless religion,' Chadwick concluded, 'but he will tremble when we pray.'

When he wound up his letter to the Ephesians, Paul included a strong stimulus to prayer. 'And pray in the Spirit on all occasions with all kinds of prayers and requests. With this in mind, be alert and always keep on praying for all the saints', Paul piled up references to prayer (Eph. 6:18). It is so easy for us to neglect true intercession in favour of gossip and giving advice. The speaker had it right who said, 'When you cannot sleep, do not count sheep; talk to the Shepherd.' Paul was insistent that the Ephesians talk to the Shepherd on his behalf.

In his final letters to Timothy Paul again returned to the subject of prayer. 'I urge, then, first of all, that *requests, prayers, intercession and thanksgiving* be made for everyone,' and the apostle became specific, 'for kings and all those in authority' (1 Tim. 2:1). No one subject soaks up more ink and hot air than politics. Like everyone else, Christians can fume for hours over the government and its failings. However, the Scripture urges us to pray for political powers. Sidlow Baxter underlined this necessity to pray for the powerful, and he added, 'The greater the diameter of our knowledge of human need, the larger will be the circumference of our petitions.'

A final Pauline reference to petition in prayer came in his last letter to Timothy. As he handed over his work to Timothy, and Timothy to God's keeping care, Paul wrote, 'I thank God . . . as I constantly remember you in my prayers (2 Tim. 1:3).

Many great hymns capture the concept of powerful prayer petition. None is more potent than the poem by John Newton (1725—1807):

> Come, my soul, thy suit prepare,
> Jesus loves to answer prayer:
> He himself has bid thee pray,
> Therefore will not say thee nay.
>
> Thou art coming to a King,
> Large petitions with thee bring:
> For his grace and power are such,
> None can ever ask too much.

---

1. See: *Living Words in Ephesians*, p. 132 and *Living Words in 1 Peter*, p. 93.
2. See: p. 15.

28.
The whole truth

'Whatever is true... think about such things' (Phil. 4:8)

Nothing but the Truth was the unusual name of a Christian musical group on the south coast during the seventies. Their label arose from their occupation, for two of the members were solicitors. The 'truth' they told was God's truth, and a very effective job they did.

It seems that truth is often sacrificed on the altar of expedience. One wartime leader of a large nation said, 'The victor will never be asked if he told the truth.' You might expect his name. It was Adolf Hitler (1889—1945). On the other side of the same war was the United States. A famous post-war president also referred to truth. 'Let us begin by committing ourselves to the truth — to see it like it is, and tell it like it is,' this great crusader for credibility cried. Then he committed himself to 'find the truth, to speak the truth and to live the truth'. His name? Richard Millhouse Nixon.

Bold contrast cries out at us when we turn to the Scriptures. For when the Bible includes the word 'truth', there is the reassuring ring of reliability about it. In fact, the Greek word used for 'truth' (*aletheia*) is used to describe upright men and women, verifiable verbage or pure metals. God's truth is sterling like silver and twenty-four carat like gold and flawless like a diamond. All of these ideas are wrapped up in the biblical word 'truth'.

In his concluding remarks to the Philippian friends, Paul points out several standards of Christian thinking. Atop the list is our word 'true' (*alethe*). 'Whatever is true, whatever is noble, whatever is right, whatever is pure, whatever is lovely, whatever is admirable — if anything is excellent or praiseworthy — think about such things' (Phil. 4:8). When the Presbyterian professor Robert Johnstone of Edinburgh lectured on the book of Philippians, he said, 'All the graces are in choral order and festal array' and truthfulness comes first.[1]

In everyday life truth is a precious commodity. It is as scarce as gold and as enduring as precious stones. When we recently visited the United States a furore was flaming away in the media. It had as its spark the 'polygraph' or lie detector. Seemingly some firms were requiring new employees to take a lie-detector test to establish their character. This I found doubly sad. First, it was a commentary on the scarcity of honesty in that society. Second, it was opposed by many employees who considered pilfering a perk of the working world. You can test for truth, but only God can make a man consistently credible.

Our word 'truth' turns up in one other Philippian context. In speaking of his detractors, Paul puts this plea: 'The important thing is that in every way, whether from false motives or true, Christ is preached. And because of this I rejoice' (Phil. 1:18). Apparently there were anti-apostolic forces at work in Philippi, and they preached the true gospel from false motives. The Philippian church leaders were appalled, but Paul was peaceful. False motives could not falsify the message. How often we become 'fruit inspectors'! The Lord said, 'By their fruit you will recognize them' (Matt. 7:16). Jesus was judging the false prophets, but we like the idea so much we wield it against all other Christians, especially those who disagree with us. It seems we need a dose of apostolic tolerance to see that God's truth is bigger than our puny little minds.

Paul urged his fellow-travellers towards heaven to fasten on truth, but he made it abundantly clear that God alone was the source of that truth. So we turn to the truth of God's Word as the criterion for all other truths, partial or pretended. It is this absolute truth that colours our considerations here.

To tell the truth

Truth has many applications in the New Testament. The first focus of truth is *God*. Jesus described his Father as 'the only true God' (John 17:3). The Thessalonian Christians were distinguished because they 'turned to God from idols to serve the living and true God' (1 Thess. 1:9). Whether under the old covenant or the new, the fact is woven through the fabric of Scripture. All idols are pretend gods: only the God of the Bible is the true God. Do you recall the bombshell exploded by Bishop John A. T. Robinson? In 1963 he unleashed his book, *Honest to God,* which was a very one-sided view of God in which the bishop tried to sap the supernatural out of the Saviour. No bishop has a corner on the Creator. The only true view of God is the Bible view. There he is seen as the only true God, unique in his character and his characteristics.

A second and predictable use of our word, 'true', is in relationship to the *Lord Jesus Christ*. According to the prologue of John's Gospel, 'Grace and truth came through Jesus Christ' (John 1:17). Jesus called himself 'the way and the truth and the life' (John 14:6). Knowing Christ is knowing the Truth, and this liberates one from sin's slavery (John 8:32). Jesus was so transparently true that the Pharisees resisted him. It is this unassailable truth that confronts many cynics. Was it not C. S. Lewis who said he was hounded by God's grace until he 'reluctantly gave in'? As I recall, he said, 'No more reluctant convert was ever dragged kicking and screaming into the kingdom.'

The third application of truth is the *Holy Spirit*. He is called 'the Spirit of truth' (John 15:26), or, again, the Spirit of truth . . . He will guide you into all truth' (John 16:13). Again in his First Epistle John denominates the Holy Spirit as the 'Spirit of truth' (1 John 4:6). His predominant characteristic, then, is truth. Whatever he teaches us is true, and the Spirit's exposition of the Saviour and the Scriptures is utterly reliable.

It is remarkable that the Spirit of truth soon shows a new convert what is true and what is not. Following a

Sunday service I was approached by a good-looking young man. He quickly explained that he was a new Christian who had been living in a homosexual relationship. His spiritual instincts (the Holy Spirit in him) told him it was wrong, and he could not understand the 'gay' Christians whom he met. He had discerned by divine direction that 'gay' and Christian were contradictory.

One further reference to truth is the *Scriptures*. When writing to the Ephesians Paul presented the 'word of truth, the gospel of your salvation' (Eph. 1:13). When Christians were taught, the basis of their beliefs was the truth in Christ Jesus (Eph. 4:21). For this reason Paul pressed young Timothy to be diligent in aspiring to God's approval as a craftsman who correctly works in the 'word of truth' (2 Tim. 2:15). Now the point is this: Scripture is equated with the Word of God and is seen as being absolutely true.

How things have changed! A minister visited one of his church members. After tea and talk he offered to read the Bible, and the elderly matron presented a Bible cut to shreds. 'What's this?', the perplexed parson puzzled.

'You see,' explained the logical lady, 'every time you have said a verse was not in the original or not reliable I simply snipped it out.' The result: shredded Scriptures.

Never turn from the truth. It originates from the God of truth. All truth is God's truth. He mediated it to the world through the Lord Jesus, the Truth incarnate. Now the Holy Spirit continues the task as the Spirit of truth. Where do I get all this? From the Word of truth, the Bible.

---

1. R. Johnstone, *Lectures on Philippians*, p. 375.

29.
Horn of plenty

'I know what it is to have **plenty***'* (Phil. 4:12)
'Whether living in **plenty** *or in want'* (Phil. 4:12)

When I think of plenty, I think of water. As a lad we used to visit Grandma Detzler's farm. (Grandpa lived there, too, but I always thought of it as Grandma's farm.) 'Farm' was a bit of an exaggeration. The land was worn down to a frazzle. Any livestock, cattle, pigs, chickens, were rather sparse and scruffy. The farmhouse was a wooden dwelling that just grew like Topsy. But it was Grandma's farm, and I loved it. In the kitchen was a gallon pail, porcelain and clean. And in it was clear, cold thirst-quenching water, which we used to drink from a large dipper. The hitch was that several times each day we had to draw water from the well outside. What a treat it was when my dad drilled a deep well (by hand) and brought an unlimited supply of water right into the kitchen! There was plenty and luxury in that simple well.

It is this picture of plenty that we focus on here. Paul used the Greek word *perisseuo,* and it abounds with such meanings as 'abundance, excess, excellence, increase, superfluous' and just plain 'more'.

Our word crops up twice in the passage under consideration. Paul remembers times of plenty, and he is content with plenty or poverty (Phil. 4:12). To the contented person, poverty *is* plenty. As one commentator put it, contentment achieves the same result as wealth. We become rich by either possessing wealth or by losing the desire for it. Apparently the apostle knew both kinds of wealth.

Today television advertising makes sure none of us becomes complacently contented. Each evening a whole parade of products is presented to our eyes and ears. First we are told what we want, then we learn where to get it and how to pay for it with plastic money. Soon we are supporting a whole houseful of things we never needed. Plenty soon turns into a pain in the pocketbook.

Not only does Paul put this word into a material context, for he also speaks of spiritual abundance. For Philippian Christians he prays that their 'love may abound more and more' (Phil. 1:9). Here is the concept of increase, an ever-expanding abundance. During our years of ministry at Kensington Baptist Church in Bristol we learned something of this abundance. The people were absolutely straight and honest. If they liked you, you knew it. And if you displeased them, you also knew it. But it is their abundance of affection which fills my memory of the years in Bristol.

While speaking of his imprisonment Paul again took up the theme of abundance. He hoped to visit the church again, 'so that through my being with you again your joy in Christ Jesus will overflow [abound] on account of me' (Phil. 1:26). Now there is the mark of a man of God! Paul was not preoccupied with his joy, but rather with the delight of disciples at Philippi. Most of our lives orbit around the words: 'I, me, mine, myself' and 'my'. Paul was outward-looking because he was upward-looking. Some years ago I had to bury the baby of a close friend. It was a tragic event, a cot death. The investigating police officer said to the sad father, 'You will have another child soon, won't you?' Sure enough, the couple had another little lad about a year later, and soon a second followed. Their joy overflowed, as did ours.

One final feature of our word is seen in Philippians. 'I have received full payment and even more, I am amply supplied [*perisseuo*]', Paul insisted, 'now that I have received from Epaphroditus the gifts you sent' (Phil. 4:18). Here our word expresses the feeling of absolute contentment. Another translation puts it, 'I am full' (AV). For more than twenty years several churches and friends supported us as missionaries. Regularly they sent off a cheque, and even more regularly they prayed for us. Their generosity fulfilled all our needs, and we could thank them with the words of Paul: 'We are amply supplied.'

Ours is a cheerful, comforting, contenting word. It speaks of abundance of supply and absence of want. The source is the Saviour and the channels are Christians. This is truth for today, and not just the figment of first-century imagination.

Bubbling over

Let me return to water for another illustration. As a boy we spent several vacations in a small village named St Helen's, Michigan. It was so small that they almost had to widen the road to put a white line down the middle. But in the village centre was a wonderful flowing, artesian well. Every time we went back the water was still flowing cool, clear and continuous. What a picture of the plentiful provision of our providential Provider!

Our word refers first and foremost to *plentiful things*. When Jesus fed 5000, he gave everyone enough *(perisseuo)*, and there were twelve baskets of 'leftovers' (Matt. 14:20). The Lord never skimps on the supply. There is always enough and more. During our years at Bristol we often were reminded of the life and work of George Müller (1805–98). He arrived in Bristol with little and he left in the largest funeral ever seen. In between he testified to the lavish Lord who provided plenty.

Another application of our word is *virtue*. Here is what I mean. To the Romans Paul wrote about God's grace which in Christ did 'overflow [*perisseuo*] to many' (Rom. 5:15). Later on Paul spoke of God's comfort which 'overflows' through Christ (2 Cor. 1:5). Just as God gives abundance of things, he also pours out plenty of provision for our spiritual lives. Many times I have seen a loved one care for a crippled parent or partner. There is an endurance which seems to stretch beyond the breaking-point. As infirmity increases the caring family member draws deeper on the abundance of Another, the ever-caring Christ of God. Now that is virtue in abundance.

The third use of our word is *growth or increase*. Our verb is found in Dr Luke's log-book, when he wrote, 'The churches were strengthened in the faith and grew [*perisseuo*] daily in numbers (Acts 16:5). Here is abundance of belief and believers. While we were living in Bournemouth we attended a great church. When the pastor retired after nearly three decades of service, there was some anxiety about the church's future. Since then two pastors have come and the church is growing both spiritually and statistically far beyond anything the previous pastor could have projected. The Grower is God.

And this brings us to the final feature of our word. The great Agent of abundance is *God himself.* When Paul praised the Corinthian Christians, he wrote, 'This service that you perform is not only supplying the needs of God's people but is also overflowing [*perisseuo*] in many expressions of thanks to God' (2 Cor. 9:12). Only God is great enough to contain an overflow of things, virtue, increase and praise.

This extravagant expression of God is seen in a remarkable little book about Hudson Taylor. Written by Dr and Mrs Howard Taylor, the invaluable volume is called *Hudson Taylor's Spiritual Secret*[1]. The first missionary book I ever read, this one sticks with me as a masterpiece of missionary biography. Hudson Taylor (1832–1905) shared both the life and vision of his older brother George Müller. Something of the shared heartbeat is seen in Hudson Taylor's triumphant testimony: 'Flesh and heart often fail: Let them fail! He faileth not.'[2]

---

1. London: China Inland Mission, 1953.
2. As above, p. 155.

30.
The incomparable Christ

'I can do all things through **Christ** *who strengthens me'*
(Phil. 4:13, AV)

When his friend Arthur Hallam died in 1842, Alfred Lord Tennyson (1809—1892) penned his masterpiece *In Memoriam*. As he approached the conclusion Tennyson cried,

> Ring in the valiant man and free,
>   The larger heart, the kindlier hand;
>   Ring out the darkness of the land;
> Ring in the Christ that is to be.

Christ triumphant was to him the only balm for a broken heart.

The Boston bishop Phillips Brooks (1835—1893) summarized the significance of Christ when he wrote, 'Jesus Christ [is] the condescension of divinity and the exaltation of humanity.' As if to expand on the same magnificent theme, Charles Haddon Spurgeon said, 'Christ is the central fact in the world's history. To him everything looks forward or backward.'

Strike the note of Christ's name and all the harmonies of human language burst into song. Nowhere is this more true than in the New Testament. The name of Christ appears 352 times, and the apostle Paul penned 268 of them. 'Christ' is a transliteration of the Greek word *christos*, and it means 'the Anointed One, the Messiah of God'.

Most modern translations exclude the name of Christ from Philippians 4:13. In the New International Version the verse reads, 'I can do everything through him who gives me strength.' The older versions, especially the Authorized Version, include the name of Christ. If his name is absent from some of the most reliable manuscripts, he was abundantly present in Paul's mind as he wrote Philippians. In fact, the name of Christ comes up twenty-five times in this short epistle.

The coming of Christ

Frequently the apostle focuses on the coming of the Lord. When he urges purity upon the Philippian Christians, Paul enforces it by reference to the coming of Christ (Phil. 1:10). Reward for faithful service is not seen in visible success, but rather in joyful anticipation of the revelation of Christ (Phil. 2:16). Christians are liberated from the frustrations of fickle human government, because their genuine citizenship is in Christ's commonwealth (Phil. 3:20). The New Testament often links the Second Coming with the name of Christ, rather than other names of the Lord. It may well be that this focus features the prophetic fulfilment of Christ's messianic mission.

At any rate, the Christian garners much comfort from Christ's coming back to earth. In my childhood during the Second World War, we were often frightened by the scourge of Fascism and Japanese imperial power. Another generation has grown up, and they fear the mushroom-shaped cloud of nuclear threat which hangs over our world. This has given birth to peace movements world-wide. The Christian knows that the climax of history is not a holocaust triggered off by some nervous politician. History will wind up when God says so, and it will usher in a time of divine dominance unknown since Eden.

Communion with Christ

A second spotlight shines on the communion which Christians share with Christ and other Christians. Paul's prison persecution simply demonstrated his nearness to Christ and Christ's companionship with him (Phil. 1:13). In fact, Paul's whole life was bound up with Christ, and he knew this to be an eternal relationship which would not be dented by death (Phil. 1:20–23). As he plodded through the Roman world of his day, Paul's physical vision was arguably weak. His spiritual sight was flawless, as he looked forward to Christ calling him 'heavenwards' (Phil. 3:14).

Recently a major television network erupted in well-publicized insults and purges. One by one familiar faces were scrubbed from the screen by an organizational abrasive, a media hatchet man. In utter frustration one of the victims turned the tools of her trade to smear the responsible official. Finally at a party she flung a glassful of wine in the ex-boss's face. 'My only regret', said she, 'was that the wine was white. I wish it had been red.' When pressed for her reasons, this articulate lady lamented, 'He has ruined my life.' What a contrast this presents! A wealthy, successful anchor-person protests that her life is over. Meanwhile the apostle Paul praises God from his prison cell, because Christ has lavished riches upon him. Communion with Christ is better company than any television network there is.

Commitment to Christ

Another aspect of Christ in Philippians is the commitment which he calls forth. Because of his own experience, Paul prepares the Philippians to suffer for Christ's sake (Phil. 1:29). No loss can ever rob the apostle of the benefits which bubble from commitment to the living Lord Jesus Christ (Phil. 3:7,8). Apparently he lost everything to become a believer. Family, friends, finance, even his religious position were sacrificed, but Christ outweighed them all. Stack all the honours man can give on one side of the scale and place Christ on the other side: Christ will counterbalance the lot.

This attitude has marked great Christians from the first. 'Jesus Christ will be Lord of all or not Lord at all,' claimed the consummate Christian thinker Augustine. In our day a similar statement came from the lips of 'the Doctor', our beloved Dr Martyn Lloyd-Jones (1899—1981). In his distinctive style of evangelism, he said, 'You can't receive Christ in bits and pieces.' Commitment to Christ is a matter of all or nothing at all.

Commissioned by Christ

One of the hallmarks of Paul's preaching was a sense of commission by Christ. He was surrounded by false preachers. Some preached a false gospel and Paul aimed Galatians at them. Others preached a true gospel for false reasons, and these Paul tolerated, because he believed the Word worked despite the spiritual poverty of its preachers (Phil. 1:15—18). When Christ is proclaimed he does the work, not some persuasive preacher.

This commission embraced all believers. Their commission was twofold. First their lives were to be worthy of the gospel of Christ. Second they were to stand firm for the faith in hand-to-hand combat with the Christless forces of their day. Word and work are not alternatives. They are two sides of the same coin of commission to serve Christ.

Some months ago a lady professed faith in Christ and confessed him in baptism. Her testimony has expanded almost daily and her knowledge of the Lord is transforming her life. She represents the fruition of teaching and training she received as a child in George Müller's orphanage half a century ago. Her deeds and her declaration adorn the gospel of Christ and colour his name with glory.

The cross of Christ

The Master's mark was on Paul. He was enamoured with Christ, and this salted all his speech and writing with the name that is above every name (Phil. 2:9). The cross of Christ alienated the whole world from Paul (Phil. 3:18), but one man with Christ is a majority.

31.
Yes, please

'An acceptable sacrifice, **pleasing** *to God'* (Phil. 4:18)

What pleases you? At the end of a long day I arrive home with a hankering. Quietly I pry open the refrigerator and take out two jars: one with jam, and the other with peanut butter. Then I liberally spread bread with brown butter and red jam. The first bite is sheer delight, and the sandwich sticks to my ribs all night. Most of my friends know that peanut butter and jam please me. On the other hand, it is a mountain of salad that pleases my wife. She, too, starts with the refrigerator, but she builds a mound of green crispness before topping it with cucumber, tomatoes, a dash of radish and a liberal lacing of salad cream. No wonder she fights a less dramatic battle with the bulging waist than I do, because salad pleases her!

It is the little word 'please' that forms the focus of this chapter. In Greek it is the word *arestos*, and it is sometimes lengthened by adding a prefix, *euarestos*, 'well-pleasing'. Although the word is sometimes applied to people, such as pleasing the Jews (Acts 12:3) or slave-masters (Titus 2:9), our word usually concerns pleasing God.

Only once does our word occur in Philippians, and it is the enlarged form, 'well-pleasing'. Paul commends the Christians for their compassion towards him. Their gifts sent with Epaphroditus are 'a fragrant offering, an acceptable sacrifice, [literally] well-pleasing to God' (Phil. 4:18). In other words, when we help out God's people, God is pleased.

In the paragraph under consideration, there are three major reasons why it is good to give aid to God's people. First, Christian giving awakens *gratitude*. 'It was good of you', Paul wrote, 'to share in my troubles' (Phil. 4:14). The reason for Paul's praise is because his fellow-believers were true friends in need. For many years we were missionaries, and our particular society identified givers by name. Thus we were able to thank personally each one who gave to support us. Retired people on fixed incomes often gave towards our work, as did young couples just starting out in life. Although we had very little 'trouble' we are thankful for those who shared with us.

A second reason for Christian giving is *eternal reward*. In this passage Paul mixes up the metaphors. He assures the Philippians 'that fruit may abound to your account' (Phil. 4:17, AV). Although they may see no visible results, God keeps the books in the heavenly treasury. Just as interest increases a savings account, so Christians collect spiritual interest from their investments in God's people and plans. One thinks of the spiritual savings of George Müller. He not only provided a home for hundreds of orphans, but he also gave by faith to many missionary enterprises. His friendship and fellowship in the work of Hudson Taylor is a matter of spiritual record. The reward of Müller is not only the memory of many Christians but also the eternal glory of his God.

The final reason for Christian giving is the *glory of God*. Our assistance to aid others is here described as an offering to God, 'a fragrant offering, an acceptable sacrifice, *pleasing* to God' (Phil. 4:18). Quite obviously we are not saved by our sacrifice, but rather by the sacrifice of our Saviour. On the other hand, we do serve Christ by sacrifice, and this alone pleases God.

How to please God

From the first people have tried to please God by the wrong means. Martin Luther thought he could please God by a painfully long pilgrimage to Rome. It did not work! Karl Marx thought he could please God by mastering great chunks of the Bible. His plan also did not work!

So what *does* please God? First, the *consecration* of our lives pleases God. When we present our bodies a living sacrifice to God, this is 'holy and pleasing to God' (Rom. 12:1). As if to underline this, Paul adds, 'You will be able to . . . approve what God's will is — his good, pleasing and perfect will' (Rom. 12:2). One remembers many martyrs who have demonstrated this. Recently I again read of John and Betty Stam, who were slaughtered in 1934 by Communist insurgents in China. They had spent less than three years in China as missionaries of the China Inland Mission (Overseas Missionary Fellowship). As a result of their death many more missionaries went abroad.

A second means of pleasing God is to *serve him*. Again in the book of Romans Paul touches on the theme by writing, 'Anyone who serves Christ in this way is pleasing to God' (Rom. 14:18). The God-pleasing form of service is living an exemplary life before other Christians (Rom. 14:13—17). Every pastor knows dozens who please God through their service. At Kensington we have a gardener who serves as caretaker of our church. Another brother leads a thrilling outreach to senior citizens from our inner-city neighbourhood. You read this book because a dear sister has given God her typing skills. These and many other forms of service please God.

In his Colossian letter Paul says that *fruit-bearing* pleases God. 'Live a life worthy of the Lord, and . . . please him in every way: bearing fruit in every good work' (Col. 1:10). Fruit-bearing is demonstrated in two ways. When Christians live for God, they bear the fruits of righteousness. Another form of fruit-bearing is winning others to Christ. When baptismal candidates present themselves, we often ask them how they came to know Christ. Usually they mention some Christian who helped them on the way. We know that other Christian was only an instrument in God's hands, but he or she was surely an instrument who pleased God. An apple tree does not bear fruit because apples are stuck to the tree with sticky-tape. Fruit flourishes naturally, and so does spiritual fruit spring from the Spirit's presence.

The great chapter of Hebrews 11 gives us another

prescription for pleasing God through *faith*. 'Without faith it is impossible to please God,' according to the writer of this landmark letter (Heb. 11:6). As we see people profess faith in Christ and live for the Lord, we know they are pleasing to God. Recently a young secretary survived a spiritual struggle when she came to faith in Christ. She had many signposts on the way, but they all pointed to Christ and pleased God.

Another activity and attitude that pleases God is *worship*. 'So worship God acceptably', says the New International Version (Heb. 12:28). To put it literally, 'We worship God and this pleases him.' In our fellowship is a former missionary who bears a burden for worship. Wherever he goes and whatever he says, worship soon seeps into the conversation, and this pleases God.

At the end of Hebrews we learn that *caring* pleases God. 'Do good and . . . share with others', the writer urges, 'for with such sacrifices God is pleased' (Heb. 13:16). Judaism has always distinguished itself by charity. During the Nazi holocaust Jews sacrificed their lives for one another, and in other lands they cared for thousands of refugees. Christians, too, are characterized by caring, and this pleases God.

In his First Epistle, John says *obedience* pleases God. 'We obey his commands and do what pleases him', the apostle concludes (1 John 3:22). No believer can adequately please God unless he obeys all the known commands of Christ. At the end of our ministry at Bristol we had the opportunity of baptizing several; one was an elderly lady from our fellowship. After many years she had concluded that baptism was necessary to a life of obedience. A joyful coincidence was the baptism that evening of her son.

Every Christian's aim is to please the Lord. This is part of the new life which Christ generates in our old bodies. It is no wonder that Paul instructed the Ephesian Christians to 'find out what pleases the Lord' (Eph. 5:10).

32.
God's glory

'According to his **glorious** *riches in Christ Jesus'* (Phil. 4:19)
'To our God and Father be **glory** *for ever and ever'* (Phil. 4:20)

It is the biblical word 'glory' that here catches our eye. 'Glory' in Greek is *doxa*. You see it in such English words as 'doxology', 'a liturgical formula to praise God'. Another twist to the term is 'orthodoxy', and it arises from two terms: *ortho* 'straight' and *doxa* 'opinion'. So we could well conclude that 'glory' is what God thinks of himself and how we should think of him too.

The word 'glory' comes up six times in Philippians. In the final chapter, Paul's conclusion, 'glory', is tied up with God's supply of our needs. He gives us all we need according to his riches in glory, or as the New International Version puts it, 'according to his glorious riches' (Phil. 4:19). When our needs are met in Christ Jesus, God is *glorified* as a faithful Father (Phil. 4:20). In other words, when Christians depend on the Lord this brings glory to his name. Everybody sees how magnificently he supplies and shares in giving glory to God.

Think of the great men of faith. Charles Haddon Spurgeon preached eloquently and thousands were saved to God's glory. His contemporary Hudson Taylor took the same gospel into the heart of China, and God got the glory. Their friend George Müller built a home for hundreds of orphans and this, too, glorified God. So the ultimate benefit was neither conversion, nor mission, nor care of orphans, but God's greater glory.

Now let us survey the glory of God in Philippians. When Christians demonstrate the *fruit of righteousness* in their lives, God is glorified. It says so in Philippians 1:11. Recently a former drunk, drug addict and criminal preached at our church. His biblically based preaching blessed us all, and his transformed life glorifies his God and ours.

Another avenue of glory is the *resurrection of Christ*. Through his resurrection God has glorified him, and our ascription of adoration underlines this glory. We declare that Jesus Christ is Lord, 'to the glory of God the Father' (Phil. 2:11). In our day there are many new scriptural choruses which lift one's eyes to the Lord and give a new glimpse of glory. One of my favourites is founded on Philippians 2:11:

> He is Lord, he is Lord,
> He is risen from the dead
> And he is Lord.
> Every knee shall bow,
> Every tongue confess
> That Jesus Christ is Lord.
> (Arranged by Norman Warren 1980.)

And that chorus gives God glory for his resurrection power as performed through Christ.

There is even a perverted glory. People who fashion their own gods turn their glory into their shame (Phil. 3:19). Recently we visited a home where death had occurred. The daughter of the deceased had resolutely resisted the call of God, and she persisted in the face of her father's death. The confused opinions which she spewed out were a travesty of truth, and the glory of God was completely absent from that conversation.

A final reference to the glory of God is seen in connection with the resurrection. Jesus is raised from the dead, and he will fit us out with a body 'like his glorious body' (Phil. 3:21). Glory and resurrection are inextricably linked in the Lord. And the glory of Christ's resurrection will be reflected in the glory of our resurrection. All of this is connected to the 'Son rise', for the Son of God is risen and he will raise us, too.

God's glory

Spread the glory

Man-made glory is as perishable as man is. In his famous 'Elegy written in a Country Churchyard,' Thomas Gray (1716—71) concluded with irrefutable logic: 'The paths of glory lead but to the grave.' Writing three hundred years earlier in Latin, Thomas à Kempis (1380—1471) blazed the same trail of despair when he wrote, 'How quickly does the glory of the the world pass away!'

In contrast to this dismal decree against man's glory stands the glory of our God. From the settling of the Shekinah glory on the tabernacle in the desert to the presence of God's glory in our worship, the glow is undimmed. God is still glorified in the praise of his people, and God is the only valid object of glory.

God the Father commands glory. When Christ came to earth the angels sang, 'Glory to God in the highest' (Luke 2:14). When Paul propounded the truth of believers' baptism he saw in it a reflection of the resurrection of Christ 'through the glory of the Father' (Romans 6:4). The sum of sacred history is calculated to cause glory to be given to God. Some years ago a brilliant medical man learned the doctrines of God's grace. As he pondered them he became increasingly convinced. Someone asked why he believed them. The consultant replied, 'Any teaching that gives glory to God must be right.' Now that is a good enough measuring rod for any doctrinal tenet.

Christ is also worthy of glory. When he came to earth his disciples were dazzled by his glory. Half a century later John wrote, 'We have seen his glory, the glory of the one and only Son, who came from the Father' (John 1:14). Then Jesus did his first miracle and brought alive the sagging marriage feast at Cana. But the reason for this miracle was to reveal 'his glory, and his disciples put their faith in him' (John 2:11). Everywhere Jesus went he spread glory around. One remembers how he took the disciples, three of them, up to a hilltop. There they prayed and relaxed, so much so that Peter fell asleep. When the former fisherman opened his eyes he was amazed, for Jesus glowed with glory. Peter babbled about building a Bible conference ground, but Christ concentrated on the glory (Luke 9:28—36).

And the *Holy Spirit* is also crowned with glory. He is the one who infects us with 'ever-increasing glory' and transforms us into the image of Christ (2 Cor. 3:18). It is also the Holy Spirit who is called by Peter the 'Spirit of glory' (1 Peter 4:14). The glory of God's Spirit is seen in many great revival movements. Think of that magnificent movement of the sixteenth century when Luther, Calvin, Knox and a score of others were used to light up the Dark Ages. A couple of centuries later it was Wesley, Whitefield, Howell Harris and Jonathan Edwards who reflected God's glory over two continents. And so it goes down through the history of God's people as the Holy Spirit ignites men and women and they ignite his people.

But God also gives glory to *his people*. The fruitfulness of Christians reflects God's glory (John 15:8). When Christians think and speak alike, this too glorifies God (Rom. 15:6). In fact, the Christian sees his body as an instrument to glorify God (1 Cor. 6:20). All of this points to the day when Christians will be glorified with Christ in his glory (Rom. 8: 17, 18, 30).

When the former president of Wheaton College died in 1967, his funeral service took place in the massive Edman Chapel. In addition to eulogies and the preaching of the Word, there was great singing. A student choir sang Handel's 'Hallelujah Chorus', and the whole congregation sang his favourite hymns, one of which contained the lines:

> My sinful self my only shame,
> My glory all the cross.
> (Elizabeth C. Clephane, 1830—69.)

What a way to go, with the glory of Christ's cross firmly fixed before one's eyes!

Other books in this series

by

Wayne Detzler

LIVING WORDS IN I CORINTHIANS

Wayne Detzler

The author, in his warm, pastoral style, surveys the main themes of Paul's First Epistle to the Corinthians, and presents thirty-three word studies packed with relevant, challenging issues.

"A further volume of sharply pointed and pungently expressed word studies."
                                    Christian Arena

"Dr Detzler . . . makes full use of illustrations in order to emphasize the truths to which he draws attention in these helpful pages. I Corinthians is shown throughout to be thoroughly up-to-date, and to meet the situations of 1984."
                                    English Churchman

LIVING WORDS IN EPHESIANS

Wayne Detzler

"Seldom has a more useful and edifying book come into my hands . . . No one at any level of Christian growth and experience could fail to be helped and thrilled by this eminently useful book."
                              Evangelical Times

" . . . combines exegetical skill, racy and attractive presentation and overall biblical balance."
                              Christian Graduate

"A first-class study book"
                              Methodist Recorder

"Dr Detzler's treatment of each text is competent, relevant, thought-provoking and spiritually edifying; altogether it is a most lively, readable and refreshing series of studies. The book is full of concise, clear explanations of Greek words and it abounds with topical references and lively illustrations."
                              Evangelical Magazine of Wales

LIVING WORDS IN I PETER

Wayne Detzler

"Here is another excellent book of word studies from Wayne Detzler . . . the reader cannot fail to be helped by what he has written."
Evangelical Magazine of Wales

"This book will have many uses. It will appeal to preachers looking for material to stimulate pulpit preparation. It will also prove helpful to leaders of Bible Study groups and in private devotional reading."
Church of England Newspaper

"All, ministers especially, would benefit from reading this book, which we heartily recommend."
English Churchman

"The book has a pastoral emphasis which, combined with its scholarly insights and apt illustrations, makes it a very readable book for any believer."
Fellowship Magazine